Busy Bee: Queen Bee

Stop the Busy Work and Become Queen of the Hive!

By

Elizabeth Bierbower

In memory of my beloved nephew

Ronald P. "Butch" Mellinger, taken from us far too soon. In 40 short years you touched more hearts and lives than anyone can imagine. You were and always will be loved, admired and cherished. I carry you with me, in my heart every day.

The Little Busy Bee

By Isaac Watts

How doth the little busy bee
Improve each shining hour,
And gather honey all the day
From every opening flow'rl
How skillfully she builds her cell!
How neat she spreads the wax!
And labours hard to store it well
With the sweet food she makes.
In works of labour or of skill,
I would be busy too;
For Satan finds some mischief still
For idle hands to do.
In books, or work, or healthy play,
Let my first years be passed,
That I might give for ev'ry day,
Some Good Account at last.

It is not enough to be busy.

So are the Ants.

The question is:

What are we busy about?

Henry David Thoreau

Table of Contents

Introduction

A Very Busy Bee

I used to be a Busy Bee. Busy, busy, busy all the time. I was busy at home with cooking, cleaning, laundry and rearing a son. I was busy at work trying to climb the corporate ladder. Busy is in my DNA. Being busy equates to hard work, and I learned that working hard was how you made something of yourself. Hard work was the way to get more. Doing more was the way to get more.

Being busy permeated every aspect of my life when I was younger. I was busy with school, with Girl Scouts, a paper route and playing on the softball team. In my youth, being active or busy was an alternative to getting into trouble. Lying around the house doing nothing equated to laziness. Go play outside or just go do something were phrases drilled into me as a child. Being busy kept us out of our mother's hair. The idea of relaxation did not exist. My parents did not relax. My role models were busy all the time.

As I matured and moved out on my own, I was busy with college, and part-time jobs, then graduate school and full-time work. In addition, I was keeping a clean and well-maintained home, ensuring a hearty dinner was on the table and clothes were clean and ready to wear. Oh yes – add on taking care of a small child.

My busy life as a young adult centered on hard work, which allowed me to earn money. Spending money on activities like ordering pizza, buying prepared foods or eating at a fancy restaurant wasted those hard-earned dollars. Eating at home saved money and provided better nutrition. Fast was also the enemy of hard work. Items – like fast food or store-bought Halloween costumes were also not a good use of the hard-earned dollar.

Purchasing the services of a professional when, with a little bit of time and patience I could do the job myself, was an even more egregious act of throwing money down the toilet. Whether it was painting the outside of a house, raking leaves, digging a hole, planting a tree, or mowing an acre of lawn each week, manual labor was a great way to get exercise. I was born and bred a DIY person before DIY was all the rage. I was a very Busy Bee indeed, and this was only outside the office.

My work ethic made me a good employee. I came in early and stayed late. I was on a conference call at the doctor's office a few hours before my son was born! I took work home almost every evening. I worked on weekends, vacations and even on some holidays. I was so intent on getting ahead that I never said "no" at the office. I was the person you could toss almost anything to and I would figure it out somehow, and I did. I stretched myself to learn about every aspect of my business.

All my life I was a worker bee. In the hive, worker bees do exactly what you would expect. They build the hive with its honeycombed interior walls. They make the honey. The younger worker bees stay inside the hive cleaning, feeding and rearing the next generation of worker bees and, if they are privileged, they feed and care for the Queen Bee, assuming it must be a privilege to serve the Queen Bee! The older worker bees (a relative term since honey bees only live about six weeks) leave the hive looking for pollen and nectar and in the process, cross pollenate plants and are instrumental in nurturing the world's food supply. Bees are super important players in the ecosystem, and their short lives are nothing but hard work. Do these routines sound familiar to you? I know I spent too many years in worker bee mode but eventually that would change.

One day very early in my career, I was whining about how my role consisted of a hodgepodge of duties. My title was Supervisor of Public Programs. The CEO and CFO of my company at the time set me straight. They told me I was lucky to be gaining the type of experience necessary to become a president or CEO of a company someday. Their feedback hit me like a lightning bolt! I thought WOW! LUCKY ME! I took their advice literally and ran with it. I immediately stopped my whining and continued on my quest to learn more, do more, and be more.

I became a zealot and was certainly more than a little unbalanced in my quest to become a leader. Yes, the advice about having a broader view of the industry would benefit me in my career, but what I failed to realize was that doing more does not automatically equal success. You have likely heard the phrase "working hard is not the same as working smart," and I found this statement to be very true. I did not realize at the time that these men had wives who did not work outside the home. They didn't have to worry about ninety percent of the home activities I had to worry about, and double that amount because I was also a single mother at the time. I will be eternally grateful for the advice I received from them that day, but it took me a long time to understand more is not necessarily better and, in fact, just the opposite is true. Less is better. Less allows you to focus on what really matters at work and at home. Less allows you to recover from a busy day or a week of travel. Less allows you to appreciate people and experiences over things. Once I began to understand doing less could give me more and still help me feel fulfilled, I began to shift my thinking and my actions from being the Busy Bee to becoming a Queen Bee.

The Queen Bee has one major role, to lay many, many eggs, in the hive. The Queen Bee lays somewhere approximately 2,000 eggs, which is a tremendous amount of pressure. The Queen Bee is the key to the next generation of bees, and the other bees treat her with great care. From the time she is a tiny larva, the

Queen Bee consumes only royal jelly, which allows her sexual organs to develop fully. She does not spend time doing the busy work. She does not make the hive, clean the cells of the honeycomb or produce the honey. The Queen Bee does not go out into the world looking for food nor does she handle any of the care and feeding of the other bees. Her job is to mate with as many male bees as possible (sounds a bit exhausting) and then lay as many eggs as possible. She avoids any activity that impedes her ability to reach her full potential. She knows what it takes to be Queen Bee, and she will do everything in her power to ensure nothing gets in the way of her achieving her goal. She'll even kill other virgin queens who are competing to become Queen Bee but I do not recommend this action! The Queen Bee is born to do less and she's good at it. You can be, too.

If you are reading this book, I assume that you, like me, want to be a Queen Bee. The definition of a Queen Bee varies based on the source. Some say is it a woman of power. Others tie the term to junior high behavior. My definition of a Queen Bee is someone who has control over her life, someone who takes charge of and cares for herself. Ultimately, you and you alone determine the definition for Queen Bee. While I have written this book from the perspective of someone who chose the corporate path, you may have a different goal in mind. You may want to be an awesome Queen Bee stay at home mother or the Queen Bee of a small business. You may be an aspiring Queen Bee artist or a Queen Bee scientist. No matter what type of Queen Bee you choose, one fundamental truth exists. Being a Busy Bee will not earn you the position of the Queen Bee. This book will show you how Busy Bee thoughts and actions can hinder your personal and professional life, and will guide you toward (appropriate) Queen Bee behavior.

My goal was to be a corporate Queen Bee. I wanted to prove at each step of the way that I could play an important role in a larger organization. I have worked hard, and have made sacrifices, some of which were meaningful and others that were really just simple trade-offs. I have been calculating when needed, and have had luck at my back on my journey. At the end of the day, I used the value of hard work, intuition, book and street smarts to get ahead and I have had a great career. Getting out of the Busy Bee mindset took a long time, and in the process, I almost derailed my career. I don't want you to make the same mistakes.

At one critical point in my career, I realized the Busy Bee mentality was working against me. I held the title of vice president in a large organization. I hear you saying, "Wait a minute, you *were* a Queen Bee!" but please continue reading. I was literally killing myself working weekends and evenings, and on more than one occasion, I was in the office past midnight. My leader at the time continued to add projects to my plate and I was feeling good, until I noticed something. More frequently, the assignments involved collaborating with another peer vice president. I was given accountability for ensuring the project was completed on time and with high quality, but once completed, I would move on to another initiative and my peer would continue running his operation (with much greater efficiency I might add)! During my time with this organization I was paid well, received above average raises and even higher bonuses for outstanding performance, but I sensed that if I did not have some operational capabilities to manage I wouldn't make it to the senior table.

I decided to discuss my observations with my leader who was a senior executive with the company. The discussion not only changed my career trajectory, it changed my life. My leader shared with me that he viewed me neither as an operator (even though I had years of successful operational experience at other companies) nor a strategic thinker (despite driving strategic projects in my current role). He quickly followed these statements with, "But you are one hell of a project manager!" I was shocked. I burst into tears on the spot, one of the few times I have ever done that. My boss could not understand why I was upset. He told me I was extremely valued, was one of the highest compensated leaders in the organization, and that everyone thought I brought a lot of value to the table. His words were not comforting and the damage irreversible. Within three months, I had another job and never looked back.

Although I was deeply hurt at the time by my leaders' views, in retrospect, I appreciate his honesty because it helped me understand I needed to change my approach to work. Had my manager not been direct me with me, I am sure I would have continued to struggle with my career. While feedback is often painful to receive it is also one of the best gifts a leader can share with an employee. However, the feedback only proves to be valuable if the receiver is willing to take the criticisms to heart. When I decided to move on from that role, it wasn't because I felt the feedback my manager gave me was wrong or unfair. I knew there was truth in what he said. However, I knew that one of my strengths was to take feedback, *learn* from it and adjust my approach. In this case, I believed having a fresh start would help me improve faster, and I was right. Whatever my current role at the time, when I received feedback, I adjusted my approach. By demonstrating to leadership that I was willing to learn and change, I was able to make continued progress in my career.

I had to demonstrate my strategic thinking skills more and pull back on my execution focus if I was going to sit at the senior table. While my transformation took a few years longer, that conversation was another defining moment for me. I finally understood that a Busy Bee does not automatically become a Queen Bee.

Over the years, I have spoken with thousands of young men and women at varying stages in their careers. I have spent time with entrepreneurs and corporate ladder types alike, sharing my journey and sprinkling my tips here and there like fairy dust. Each time I have a conversation I am told, "You have to write your experiences and advice down and share more broadly." As you will learn from this book, I rarely feel that I HAVE to do anything, but I did feel compelled to write this book for one simple reason. YOU!

In my many conversations, I see an image of my former self in others and I want share the pitfalls in trying to "have it all," hoping you will benefit from these lessons. My desire is to help you understand that "having it all" is not about "doing it all;" rather "having it all" is about making choices and quieting the Busy Bee within many of us. While my thoughts and ideas are rather simple, their execution requires both work and bravery on your part. While being a Busy Bee takes work, ceasing the busy-ness also requires work. Your Busy Bee personality comes from developing a set of habits over years. Habits are not easily changed. They require practice over time. Practice is hard work, but the more you practice, the better you become until the new habit becomes second nature to you.

As you read these pages, you will see you also have to be brave enough to be honest with yourself about what really matters to you versus what is meaningless Busy Bee activity. You'll have to muster the courage to make tough calls with your friends, co-workers and even your loved ones. Saying "NO" requires bravery. Saying "NO" is the only way to free up space for the things to which you want to say "YES." Taking time to focus on yourself when others are clamoring for a piece of your soul is brave. My hope is that you will see how you can stop being a Busy Bee in order to become the Queen Bee of your own life.

This book will help you design your *personal* life in a way that nourishes your career and your relationships by focusing on what matters and changing what doesn't – regardless of how small it seems. I'll share my personal experiences, good and bad, my choices, right or wrong, and my methods for saying the word "NO" and sticking with it. You will read examples of the many activities I have chosen to outsource, automate, or stop altogether. Independently, each one of these activities is small, but collectively they add up and can result in freeing up a significant amount of time in your personal life. This book focuses on improving your personal life as a means to providing you with the time and energy to get to where you want to be professionally. While I share many "aha" moments tied to my career, I won't actually give you career advice since there are many good books and articles available on that topic. Maybe I will save that information for the next book!

While written from a woman's point of view, I have shared my perspective with many men who have adopted these techniques to simplify their lives and have found happiness with themselves, their families and their careers, so, gentlemen, this book is for you too! Even if you try only a tip here or there, I believe you will find more time for yourself, your family and your career.

A VERY BUSY BEE

Come fly with me you Busy Bee and let's see if you have what it takes to quiet the 'busy' so you can start leading the hive.

Promise me you'll always remember;

You're braver than you believe,

And stronger than you seem,

And smarter than you think

**~Said Christopher Robin
to Winnie the Pooh**

Chapter 1
Queen Bee Advice

The marketplace is flooded with books and articles telling us how to advance our careers and become better leaders. These good works tell us how to "Lean In" to our careers, take on more responsibility, and ask for the big raise or promotion. We learn the importance of having authentic conversations, effectively managing conflict and dressing for success. If we want to be more assertive, there are books that can teach us to swim with the sharks and play hardball. No doubt this wealth of information is useful in helping us pursue a successful career, but is it enough to help us achieve the success we are *truly* seeking? Will these books help you become a Queen Bee? In part, yes, because they are very good at outlining the steps required to get to the top, but they often don't provide guidance on making personal tradeoffs needed to help you on your journey to whatever you desire – a professional career, owning a business being a present and engaged mom, etc., without leaving you utterly exhausted. In other words, they don't quiet the Busy Bee inside.

The fundamental truth is that we must have control over our personal lives in order to have a successful professional life. Most career advice fails to address the chaos many of us face in our personal lives. Like the hundreds of worker bees in the hive, we have activity swirling around us constantly, yet the books that teach us how to achieve success are devoid of practical advice on how to shore up our personal lives to support our career aspirations. Lack of control in our personal lives (real or perceived) makes it extremely difficult to climb the corporate ladder, take a more interesting lateral role that might require travel or to grow our small business. As a result, many people who want a more fulfilling work life take themselves out of the game early fearing they cannot manage both the challenges of career and family. Sheryl Sandberg raised this dilemma in her book *Lean In*. She is right. Women in particular are so concerned they might not be able to balance career and family that they actually pull back from professional opportunities even before these opportunities present themselves. Imagine saying to yourself, "I will never be good at playing the piano, so I won't even try." Many women don't pursue the next rung on the ladder, convinced a step up in career means they will fail to have a fulfilling personal life. They prefer the routine of a Busy Bee because it's comfortable and they mistakenly believe that the role of Queen Bee is just too much for them.

When I pose the question, "What are your career aspirations?" there is a very good chance the response will come back as, "I don't want to be you!" Truthfully, I have had the thought at times, "I don't want to be me either!" Seriously, what do these women think I am, a

24/7 machine without a life? There were times I was close to being that person but, over time, I learned how to shift my behavior. These learnings did not come from a book on career advice. I realized that I needed to take the steps necessary to rid my life of meaningless activity and delegate basic activities that did not require my personal attention at home and work. Making these changes required a new mindset . . . a mindset of a Queen Bee.

When women tell me they don't want to be me, what I hear is that they are taking themselves out of the game before they even know the rules. They are assuming that I have no personal life. Au contraire. I have a wonderful personal life with a loving, supportive husband and a smart, nice son who actually lives in his own home and not my basement. These women assume I work every evening and weekend (I am working in the evenings but it is on this book). While this statement was accurate years ago, nothing could be farther from the truth now.

As an executive leading a multibillion-dollar division of a Fortune 100 company, you can be sure I am busy, but I am far from a Busy Bee. Unlike the earlier stages in my career, I have taken control of and streamlined my personal life. Early in my career I played by the rules – work hard, keep your head down, etc. As I grew smarter, I *changed* the rules.

I learned a good lesson from a very smart professor named Gordon Hewitt. To succeed in transforming a business, you don't play the game you *change* the game. Busy Bee: Queen Bee will help you to write your own rules *and* change the game. In turn, you will position yourself for success at home and in the workplace.

The premise of this book is simple. You must learn to effectively manage the Busy Bee activities in your personal life and recharge your batteries in order to become a successful Queen Bee for whatever passion you have. The concept is simple but the execution requires a change in mindset and a lot of practice.

Busy Bee: Queen Bee will help you take your A-game to work without losing your health, your mind, or your precious family because you have made the right choices to minimize the chaos in your personal life. This book will help you examine and simplify your personal life, and in so doing, lead to meaningful results both at work and at home.

For now, I am encouraging you to set aside all those career advice books that sit partially read on your nightstand. Get into your favorite pajamas, pour yourself a glass of wine and commit to reading this book. I promise you will find *something* that is useful. You might even find yourself smiling at my mishaps and along the way; you'll quiet that Busy Bee that lives inside of you – if only for a few hours.

"You can call me Queen Bee"

Lorde

Chapter 2
Our Personal Hives

A high percentage of the activities in our personal lives often consists of busy-ness. I don't intend this statement to be derogatory. I believe this is simply life. We have many things to do to manage our personal lives, like running a household, taking care of people such as babies and spouses, aging parents and nosy in-laws. Personal lives have more twists and turns than a soap opera with real life medical issues like simple bumps and bruises to more serious health conditions and even death. Personal lives revolve around activities such as Kaitlyn's taekwondo or Brittany's cello lessons, not to mention homework and science projects. Personal lives include fights over loading the dishwasher or folding the bath towels properly.

Reducing the busy work does not mean you have to trade in your husband or partner, but you will need to leverage your loved one. You won't have to give your kids up for adoption, although this thought *will* cross your mind when they are teenagers. You also won't have to prioritize your work life over your personal life. Freeing yourself of busy work does, require some thought, planning, and skill.

For most of us, organizing our work is not a problem. We know how to prioritize activities, or shut down unproductive initiatives to manage the limited human and capital resources available. We can efficiently ship millions of products around the world, negotiate rock-bottom pricing for services and conduct impromptu presentations to the executive team. In fact, managing work is often *easier* than managing our personal lives. I realize this statement represents a contrarian view to some people, especially if you are reading this book and have 100 emails sitting in your inbox. Think for a minute why you can accomplish these major feats at work but not at home. At work, we typically have a support system. We know where to get the information or the products and tools we need to complete a particular project. We know whom we can rely on for help.

Most businesses have a standard cadence or routine that typically allows for pre-planning. You know which day each month the books need closed or that an update is due to your manager on the third Wednesday of every month. You pre-plan for your busy season to ensure you have the needed resources to meet expectations. With your team, you can shift responsibilities and handle the most urgent issues. The same concepts apply at home. You have a busy season (beginning of the school year, holidays, etc.) and you can often anticipate your needs in advance. Additional information on pre-planning is included in Chapter 4.

While many of us have a routine in our personal lives, I do find many last-minute variables can often disrupt these routines. Take the infamous class science project. While little Julie has known about this project for the last three months, I guarantee that *you* will learn about it on a Sunday evening around 6 pm, the night before the project is due. Many thanks to my father for bailing me out year after year in this effort. If you are like most parents, your kids participate in sports activities. Sports adhere to a strict schedule that should allow for pre-planning. Unfortunately, things can change at a moment's notice. A rainstorm could rock your world by causing you to scramble to pick up little Jimmy at the school an hour earlier than planned.

Why is it that these seemingly small events wreak havoc on our personal and professional lives? Most of us prefer certainty. We like the stability of a plan. An interruption to our plan, especially on short notice, means we have limited time to figure out how to attack the problem and correct the situation. For example, sudden cancellation of a sports practice session causes you to scramble for support. Your child suddenly needs transportation home in less than an hour, your job is located 30 minutes away and your manager just called an impromptu staff meeting. Situations arising out of nowhere cause conflict because you have overlapping commitments. On the one hand, your kid needs you to ensure his safety. On the other hand, you have a commitment to your employer, not only because your company pays you a wage but also because you commit to being at work and productive in exchange for that wage. You can slip out of work early but if that happens too many times your personal brand takes a hit as your boss and co-workers assume you are incapable of taking on additional responsibilities and damaging your prospects of becoming a Queen Bee.

Another reason these personal crises seem more challenging is that many of us lack a natural support system or safety net at home. Either we don't live near our immediate or extended families, or grandma and grandpa have their own lives and aren't available at a moment's notice to step in and save the day. Finding a support system to pick up the slack in a pinch is challenging at best.

I lived near Pittsburgh Pennsylvania early in my career. The winters bring cold temperatures, sleet, and snow, which can be extremely inconvenient for those commuting to work. One morning I arrived at the day care center only to discover a "close due to inclement weather" sign on the door. Rather than drive the twenty miles back home in the snow, I decided to take my son with me to the office. I figured if he became too much of a distraction I would leave the office. This event happened long before the internet, so working remotely was a lot more challenging then. I shut my office door, laid a blanket on the floor with some toys and hoped for the best. I was feeling good for a while until the CEO knocked on my door. Of course, he understood what had transpired with the weather and was supportive, but I knew my solution was temporary. Both my parents worked at the time so they could not take care of my son. Had I known about the day care closure, I could have imposed on my sister, a stay-at-home mom with three young kids of her own. As a single parent at the time, I did not have a strong support system and I know many of you are in the same boat today. Furthermore, I failed to realize there were significant geographic limitations to my support system. No one near my place of work could assist me in the event of an emergency. Identifying a support system and always having a backup plan are a priority. I'll share more information on this topic later.

At this point, some of you are reassuring yourself you have these situations covered. Sick kid? No problem, I can nurse Jamie back to health while I am conducting a virtual meeting for a $10M project. You might be telling yourself you can and do have it all. If you really believe this type of self-talk to be true, then good for you, sister! This book probably won't help you much, but, if you have this tiny little gnawing feeling in the pit of your stomach that you are teetering on the brink of disaster most days, then please do read on!

Having it All

What does "having it all" mean exactly? Having good health? A family? A job and a comfortable home? A nice handbag? You bet. Most people want much more than material goods to define themselves and their success. Measuring your success through some materialistic means is natural. I believe is it acceptable to want nice things and I am sure you deserve them, but wanting more will cost more in terms of personal time commitments and trade-offs. You simply have to be prepared at times to make tough choices. I find many people fail to face these issues head on and make the tough decisions. As a result, they quickly become overwhelmed with meaningless busy work. Worse yet, they take themselves out of the game and fail to achieve their aspirations.

The definition of having it all has become synonymous with doing it all, and therein lies the challenge. We equate our aspirations of having more with doing more. We wear our excessive busy-ness on our sleeves like a badge of honor. We tell ourselves (and others) we only need five hours of sleep each night. We fill with pride when we tell our friends how our little girl plays the violin and the piano, plays two sports, volunteers at a homeless shelter and is taking five advanced placement courses in high school. Our ego grows even more when we share that we are on two community non-profit boards, lead the PTA fund raising committee, and have surpassed the million-mile club with our favorite airline. We overschedule our family and ourselves, and we are depleting our most precious resource – our health. A life worth living is not about more, it is about less. Having a good life is about focusing on *the right things rather than all things.*

No Queen Bee has it all. This insect has a singular focus: mate and then lay eggs. She can't just pop out of the hive and gather nectar from flowers for fun. If she doesn't maintain this focus, the colony does not survive. Many people look at celebrities as having it all. Look more closely and you will see many of them are divorced, have drug, alcohol or behavioral health issues within their families, are overweight, and on and on. Something always has to give, but if you make wise choices, your personal life does not have to suffer.

Don't get nervous. I am not asking you to step off the career ladder, slow the growth of your business or not follow your personal passion. I want you to be able to grow professionally, earn more money to buy a house, put your kids through college and meet your personal goals. You work hard so you deserve these things and more, but I am going to ask you to make smart choices about what really matters to you. Through the conscientious act of choosing what is important, you can create success at work and home. Every day you make decisions at work to focus on which project or activity requires your undivided attention. We simply need to transfer these skills to our home life. Understanding the importance of making choices and then following through in the right way will enable you to succeed at work and home without guilt and stress.

Are you still not convinced? Are you telling yourself you have everything under control? Really? Again, good for you! However, if you are like many of the women and men I speak with every day who stress over their work and home life, you may be one-step away from having that rung on the career ladder break beneath the pressure.

Try this quick quiz to see if you are juggling too much.

- You routinely get less than seven hours of sleep each night.

- You and your spouse/partner divide duties on the weekend to get things done and are apart for four or more hours in a day.

- You have missed your kid's soccer goal, home run, etc. because you were texting, checking email or on a conference call.

- You have purchased baked goods such as a cupcake or pie and passed them off as homemade.

- You have purchased a costume at the local drug store within 24 hours of "Trick or Treat."

- You have snuck your kid into the office due to the unexpected lack of daycare.

- You are afraid to tell anyone at work you are caring for a loved one for fear of missing the next promotional opportunity.

- You feel like you are disappointing everyone.

- You constantly experience symptoms of stress such as your mind racing or your chest hurting.

If you answered "yes" to any one of these questions, then you might be setting yourself up for a big fall down the road. Sadly, I can answer "yes" to every one of these questions. The good news, though, is that this was all in the past. I have taken the steps necessary to avoid situations that cause me undue anxiety and stress. You can, too.

Unstructured or Too Structured

Our personal lives can often be chaotic. You might think a lack of structure causes this chaos and that certainly can be the case. However, chaos can also result from being overly structured. Let's look at both extremes.

Messy lives typically arise due to a lack of structure, literally as well as figuratively. Take a typical family with two school aged kids and a dual income household. We will call them the Greenberg family. The Greenberg kids wake up and have to decide in the morning what to wear. Further complicating matters, most of their clean clothes are in the laundry room rather than in their closets. Breakfast is whatever they can grab and carry with them. The kids search to find their backpacks and schoolwork and it's likely they will be late to the bus stop, which means Mom, or Dad will have to drive them to school and risk being late for work.

Now let's look at the Sanjay family with a single head of household. Their mom has planned to avoid the morning rush. The kids are required to lay out their school clothes the night before. They have also packed their own lunches, a process made much easier with the food prep that Mom did over the weekend. Breakfast is a no brainer since Mom has placed two bowls, spoons, cereal and some extra snack bars on the counter as a signal to eat breakfast. The Sanjay kids are required to collect all their schoolwork each night and place their backpacks on the hooks near the kitchen door, eliminating the need to search for their backpacks in the morning. Mama Sanjay has placed part of her children's allowance at stake if they fail to do these basic tasks. (Bribery is perfectly acceptable for children as a means to help them create good habits).

The morning rush is so much easier when you take the time to bring a little bit of structure into your life. Some advance planning and light organizational skills will help you navigate the everyday activities of life much easier. Everyone in the Sanjay family gets their day started on the right foot while you can imagine that the Greenberg family is beginning their day with tension. Notice that Ms. Sanjay focused on the Busy Bee activities that would yield her family the most effective morning routine. She prepared food over the weekend so her children could pack their lunches without issue. She also identified a few small activities for which she can hold her kids accountable and put a portion of their allowance at risk. The children get a good breakfast each day because she has prioritized meals in her household. When my son was young, I put the cups, plates and any other dinnerware or containers he might need in the bottom cabinets as a means to help him self-serve. This approach saved me a great deal of time and effort and taught him some basic household skills along the way.

In my career, I have witnessed many Greenberg families. I state "in my career" because these people manage their work and home lives in similar fashion. I once had a team member who simply could not make it to work on time. I will call her Julia. She always had an excuse for being late. Some days it was traffic, other days her child was ill or the alarm clock failed to ring. In addition to being late, Julia always seemed to have a cold or the flu. At work, Julia had a unique organizational system to say the least. Paperwork that needed filing piled up on top of her desk and cabinets for months at a time. I am not exaggerating. Her desk was a mess. Miraculously she knew exactly which stack of papers to look in to retrieve whatever I needed. While she met her basic tasks, her world was chaotic.

Both Julia and her husband worked and were actively involved in caring for their small child. One day I sat down with Julia to try to understand why she could not make it to work on time. She lamented for some time on how much work it took to get the child ready in the morning. I asked why she didn't consider preparing things the night before. As the conversation evolved, I learned that Julia's personal organizational skills were identical to those at work. She knew where everything was but pulling it all together in an efficient manner eluded her.

Julia was very close to her mother. Several times a week after work, Julia and her family stopped at her mother's house for a visit with the baby. From there, Julia and her family often went out to dinner because she was too tired to cook. They usually arrived at the restaurant between 7:30 and 8:00 pm. When the family returned home, the exhausted parents tucked him into bed fully clothed saving the task of giving him a bath until the next morning. Given all of the evening activities that transpired outside of the home each evening, Julia and her husband found it difficult to complete any tasks around the house during the week. Because the child did not adhere to a routine, he often caught colds that he passed to Julia and her husband as well.

I asked Julia to rethink her routine. Perhaps her mother could visit at Julia's house during the week and Julia could go to her mother's house on the weekend. The baby could get his bath with the assistance of Julia's mother thus combining the visit with the much-needed task of bathing. Rather than eating out most nights, I suggested that at least a few nights a week, Julia look at take out or prepared food from the grocery store. I encouraged Julia to speak with her pediatrician about getting the baby on a better sleeping schedule. Julia agreed to try some of the changes we discussed and she met with some success. Had Julia not made the changes, she would not have been able to keep her job.

We all have encountered people like Julia in the workplace. They are disorganized, arrive late at work, take excessive time off and make many excuses. Employees like this jeopardize their future. In Julia's case she wanted to remain in the job she was doing, which was great because she could not handle additional responsibility. Even Worker Bees inside the hive have focus. They are nurses, foragers, builders or one of a few other skilled roles. While our lives will never have a singular Worker Bee like focus, surely we can learn something from them in terms of narrowing tho activities we undertake.

From time to time, events happen in our personal lives that can derail us at work. I understand and have personally experienced this phenomenon on many occasions. However, when you are organized, you get back on track and your colleagues at work don't give you a demerit because they know this was an unexpected bump in an otherwise smooth road. When you are constantly struggling, it hurts your brand at work and this negative brand will stick with you for a very long time if not forever.

One of the things I enjoy is getting to know team members at all different levels of the organization. I usually have a quick call or a face-to-face meeting with them. You would be shocked at the number of times these individuals "forget" we have the meeting scheduled and are "no shows." To exacerbate further their faux pas, they offer up lame excuses or sometimes no excuse at all. Inevitably, unorganized individuals do not handle the recovery part well.

Recently, I had a meeting scheduled and the person was a no show. Twenty minutes into the scheduled time, I sent an email asking the individual whether the meeting was on his calendar. The response I received was, "Sorry I was late to the meeting. I will reschedule with your assistant." Firstly, the individual was not late. He was a no show. Secondly, I received no reason as to why the individual was late. I am not interested in personal details but I do want honesty. I delayed putting another meeting on my calendar with this individual and I discussed the matter with her leader. Shortly after the leader discussion, I received an email with an apology and a vague excuse. When I did reschedule the meeting, the individual failed to apologize in person. Interestingly, I received on at least one occasion less-than-stellar feedback on this individual's work ethic. Suffice it to say this individual will not receive an endorsement from me in the future.

In contrast, I had a woman fail to show up for a meeting. I texted her and she immediately texted back and said, "I blew it. I am really sorry, it's entirely my fault." While I was not happy she wasted my time, I appreciated her honesty and accountability. Later that afternoon she sent me an email telling me she had tried to come to work that day but turned back around and went home because she was very ill and in the process forgot about the meeting. She again apologized and asked permission to reschedule the meeting with my assistant.

The difference between these two scenarios is not only personal accountability, but also, underneath, you could clearly see that the first individual missed the meeting because they lacked structure. The other missed the meeting because she was truly suffering from the flu.

The signs of an unstructured life are easy to spot — lack of order, failing to complete tasks on time or not at all, and indifferent to time boundaries. Messy people cannot seem to finish what they start. For example, someone who is unstructured may make dinner but does not clean up. They do the laundry but leave the clothes in the dryer rather than folding and putting them away.

You may choose to live a chaotic life. It's your choice. If you want to succeed in your career, at building a business or following your passion, you need to find a way to organize your personal life. Messy personal lives spill over into the workplace and a telltale sign is that the messy individual will often hide behind excuses. If you have ever made one of these statements for missing an important deadline or meeting at work, and you knew you were stretching the truth just a bit, your personal life is probably in the chaotic zone:

- Traffic was a nightmare.
- The meeting is not on my calendar.

- I could not complete that project because I am still waiting on some numbers from the Finance Department.

- Marketing is still collecting the research.

- I was working on the project but Corporate called and I had to focus on that request first.

The problem with these excuses is that you are only fooling yourself. Your leader, co-workers, customers or students know when you are covering up the real issue. Offering up these types of excuses over time will hurt your work performance. Leaders look for organized people who can keep their commitments and deliver the quality of product or service expected. If you can't keep your personal life straight, who will trust you to handle significant projects or processes at the office?

On the opposite end of the spectrum, many of us are completely over scheduled. If returning to work is more relaxing than your personal life, you are overscheduled. If you don't see your spouse until 5 pm on Saturdays because you each are chauffeuring the kids in different directions, you are overscheduled and possibly on the path to exhaustion.

Most of us live in or dangerously near this zone. We place too much on our plates at home so we can feel like a good wife or mother. Why do we feel this need to be the perfect parent or spouse? Perhaps we want to be a better parent than what we felt we had or maybe our mother's voices are nagging at us, telling us to hold onto traditional roles and responsibilities. Maybe we go along with the super woman stereotype because it's less intimidating to blend in rather than feeling guilty for not fulfilling other people's expectations. Whatever your reason, it is time to stop the insanity and get control over your personal life.

Let's look at the overscheduled Diminico Family. Once again, both parents hold full time jobs and they have two school-aged children. Sam Diminico participates in track, the school newspaper and lacrosse. This level of activity doesn't seem like too much on the surface, but factor in Sam's part-time job, advanced high school classes, church attendance most Sundays, and volunteer activities and you will see that he is overscheduled. Sarah Diminico is in junior high. She plays soccer and softball, is in the STEM (Science, Technology, Education and Math) program, and takes piano lessons and volunteers weekly at a nursing home. Like Sam, she also attends church. Mom is a commercial architect and Dad runs his own small marketing business.

The Diminicos are super busy people. Including church (and, yes, this needs to be counted as a scheduled activity although an extremely important one), each child has at least four weekly activities. Furthermore, some of the sports in which the kids are involved require travel, which requires a lot of driving on the weekends. Mr. and Mrs. Diminico are taking each kid to separate activities on Saturdays, spending as many as five hours apart. The Diminico kids are also carrying an extra heavy schoolwork load that requires a significant amount of homework each night and on weekends.

The Diminicos have two demanding jobs that also require some travel and heavy client interaction resulting in late meetings and client dinners. Because they are saving for their retirement and their children's educations, the Diminicos handle their own cleaning, laundry, and grocery shopping and lawn maintenance. I feel overwhelmed just thinking about the Diminico family's schedule.

I bet the Diminico family's situation sounds familiar. Are your children's days filled with schoolwork and extracurricular activities? Do many of these activities spill over into the weekend? Add your children's workload to your work and home maintenance and you have the potential for a perfect storm. Can we possibly find time to restore ourselves when we barely have time to breathe?

Beyond the feeling of being overwhelmed, how do we determine we are overscheduled? How do we begin to take the necessary steps to get more balance? Ask yourself, do I want my life to be different? Do I want to have more time to focus on the things that matter to my family and me? Do I want to feel present with and really enjoy the time I have with my loved ones? If the answers to these questions are yes, then bravo for a great first step. You have the right mindset to begin to take action.

The next step is a small but important task. You will need to assess the current state of activities. Jot down *all* your family's activities for two weeks and I do mean everything. Capture every stop you make for coffee and groceries, your household activities, your children's activities including schoolwork and other family activities like attending church and going to Grandma's for Sunday dinner. Include activities like reoccurring telephone calls to your mother or sister, reading, gardening, spending time on social media sites and playing electronic games.

Note how much time you spend doing each activity and whether or not it is meaningful (remember just because it isn't meaningful does not mean it's not necessary), and whether you like the activity. Your journal should look like something this:

Activity	Time/ Frequency	Meaningful	Like/ Dislike	Keep/ Outsource/ Automate/ Stop/ Decrease
Pack lunch	10 min/ daily	yes	dislike	Keep
Cleaning	90 min/ weekly	no	dislike	Outsource
Pay Bills	30 min/ weekly	no	dislike	Automate
Lawn care	90 min/ weekly	no	like	Outsource
Pinterest	60 min/ daily	sometimes	like	Decrease to 30 min

As you can see from the journal above, there are many opportunities to get precious time back in your life and there are tradeoffs. Packing my lunch is not my favorite activity but it is important to eat right so I deem this as a meaningful activity and one that I will not delegate. Pinterest, on the other hand, is pure entertainment for me, which gives it some level of meaning because it takes my mind off work; however, it is not worth an hour of my time each day.

Take the time to jot down all your activities and have an open mind to freeing up time in your life. The next few chapters explain the benefits of outsourcing, automating and stopping activities.

"The Bee is domesticated but not tamed."

William Longgood

Chapter 3

Know Thyself

Providing you with ideas on what activities to curb on or stop completely is easy for me, but it will be up to you to take the steps necessary to follow through and trust me, this *is* the hard part. Over the years, I have made many commitments to myself and have not kept them. In my mind, I always had a good reason why I couldn't lose weight, just had to participate in a call on a Saturday or take on yet another assignment.

I failed to realize I did not know myself well enough to understand I would fail at most of my lofty *internal* commitments. This statement might seem strange coming from someone who leads a large division within a Fortune 100 company. Surely, I have some ability to meet internal as well as external commitments. The truth is I have always had difficulty meeting important internal expectations because my priorities centered on others and never myself. I never really understood why I could not meet critical internal commitments until I stumbled upon a book titled *Better than Before* by Gretchen Rubin. One of the chapters in this book discusses the concept of the "Four Tendencies." When I read this chapter, I understood for the first time why I constantly failed at meeting major internal commitments.

Rubin describes four different personality traits and explains how each one relates to *meeting expectations*. This approach was new to me. Over the years, I have taken many different personality assessments but I always viewed the findings through the lens of work. Am I collaborative enough? Am I a team player? Am I a leader or a follower? Aggressive or passive? I never really thought about the concept of meeting expectations. I failed to understand how I react to the expectations of myself and of others. I have been successful at work because I rarely if ever have difficulty meeting the expectations of others. I have a boss whose expectations I need to meet. I have deadlines and need to satisfy the requests of my peers and other team members. The chapter describing the Four Tendencies (which is now a book of the same name and I highly recommend reading it) allowed me to understand that the reason I could not meet lofty internal commitments such as losing weight, writing a book, etc., was because I had to be accountable only to myself and no one else. Apparently, I do not value personal commitments as much as I do commitments to others. According to the Four Tendencies, I am an *Obliger,* which means if I make a commitment to *anyone but myself,* I will likely succeed. However, I do really struggle keeping my internal commitments. Thus, I thrive at working and in doing for others outside of work, but when it comes to focusing on *me,* I often fail miserably. Coincidentally, this personality trait sounds a lot like that of a Busy Bee, take care of everyone else in the hive and in the process, literally work yourself to death. A worker bee's life is very short!

I have had a lifelong struggle with my weight, gaining, then losing, then gaining again over the years. I tried everything including Weight Watchers (multiple times), Nutrisystem, Jenny Craig, Atkins and a myriad of other diets. Every time I began a new diet, I would not tell anyone, not even my husband. The poor man had to figure out on his own I was doing something different with my diet. Why was I silent? Because deep down I knew and feared I would inevitably not succeed and then would be embarrassed at failing to lose or keep the weight off. I always had this voice of doubt telling me I could not reach the goal. It is hard to explain why I have this internal belief. It just exists within me. Couple this fear with the many excuses I had about why I could not take care of myself, and you have the DNA of a Busy Bee.

Once I read the chapter and then, subsequently, the book titled the *Four Tendencies*, I realized I would always struggle keeping longer-term commitments to myself unless I created an accountability framework to help keep me on track. I have little issue accomplishing small tasks like running errands, cleaning out the closet, etc. I can even meet some more challenging tasks like planting flowers and cleaning out the basement. Once I understood I was an Obliger, I realized my ability to meet small and short-term commitments was tied to my "to do" list and the ability to feel a great sense of accomplishment at the end of each day when I saw all those checked off tasks! Now, every day I jot down what I want to accomplish. As a result, I finish more tasks, including activities that are meaningful to me like writing this book, not just busy work. As an Obliger, I need a robust accountability structure to succeed with the bigger items like weight loss.

As I mentioned, I had joined Weight Watchers many times over the years and I lost some weight but never made it to goal. Each time I started feeling comfortable I would stop tracking and measuring and I would gain the weight back. My attitude was "I've got this!" and I believed I knew what to do and therefore, did not require the structure or support the program provided. I was so wrong. In addition, I really disliked attending Weight Watcher meetings. I would assume other meeting attendees were not in a similar situation as me with the weekly travel, sleeping in hotel rooms and ordering off unhealthy room service menus. I decided those meetings were not suitable for me so I stopped attending. Furthermore, if I had a bad week, I would avoid the weigh in. My actions were the opposite of what I needed to succeed. Attending meetings, measuring and tracking food and weighing in weekly are all accountability tools that someone like me needs in order to stay on track. The lack of these tools also demonstrated why prepared food based programs like Jenny Craig and Nutrisystem did not work for me in the long run. Once I stopped eating the prepared food I was undisciplined in controlling portions and indulged more in unhealthy than healthy foods.

In January 2015, at one of my workplace town halls, an associate asked how I was going to improve my well-being in the New Year and I blurted out, "I am going to join Weight Watchers!" When I left that meeting I thought OMG, I just committed to 3,000 associates that I was going to join Weight Watchers. Now I was going to *have* to join Weight Watchers because I would never intentionally disappoint my associates. I am such an Obliger! After reading about the Four Tendencies, I realized my public commitment to joining Weight Watchers helped me establish accountability with my associates. Every month they would see me on the webcast and be able to determine whether I was sticking with the program. It worked. Each month my associates saw me shrinking before their very eyes. I shared my progress with the associates and in turn, they gave me tremendous support and feedback. When I traveled to a field office my favorite breakfast foods, Cheerios, skim milk and fruit magically appeared. My fellow teammates *wanted* me to succeed. They were cheering me on and encouraging me every step of the way. At a recent event, the planning team included the Weight Watchers points for every type of food on the buffet. What a wonderful gesture and more importantly, the signs with the points represented a form of accountability.

I reached my goal in February 2016, and I am now a lifetime member. I continue to measure, track, weigh in weekly, and attend meetings. These tools are what helped me lose the weight, and I now realize I need them in my life in order to keep the weight off. When people see me entering my points or hear me mention attending a meeting, they often ask, "Are you still doing that program? Aren't you finished?" I always respond by explaining that adopting a healthy diet and other well-being habits is a lifetime commitment. What is most important is that *I know myself.* I now know I need tools and accountability to create success for any major personal commitment. For example, I purposely shared with colleagues that I was writing this book because I knew once my commitment was public that I would be more likely to follow through. This public statement serves as an external accountability structure for me. For smaller activities, I carry a little notebook in my purse and write down what I intend to accomplish and it is rate that I fail to complete all activities within a twenty-four hour period. I admit that I get a level of satisfaction from checking things off my list. Knowing how to hold yourself accountable will help you in your quest to quiet the Busy Bee.

Think about the Queen Bee. She knows from birth she is destined to be Queen and she does everything she needs to as a means to achieve her goal. In the case of the Queen Bee, it means she must choose not to do the tasks of the Busy Worker Bee. Rather, she must focus on eating her royal jelly and laying all those eggs. On the other hand, the Busy Bee knows her role, which is taking care of the hive and fellow bees until her short life ends. Unfortunately, too many of us fall into the Busy Bee category, but there is hope.

Understanding *whom you are* and *what you need to succeed* to stop the busy-ness will help ensure you have the necessary framework to make changes in your personal life. Whether you read Rubin's book or another self-help book, I encourage you to dig deep and understand what drives you so you can establish the right framework to succeed at stopping the Busy Bee work and getting on to the work of the Queen Bee. Let's do this!

"Believe you can and you are halfway there."

~ Unknown

Chapter 4

Pre-planning

Weight Watchers members have a saying, "Failure to plan is a plan to fail." We use this saying to prepare ourselves for an upcoming event or any other activity that might cause us to disrupt our good eating and other healthy habits. For example, when I have a client dinner, I try to choose the restaurant which ensures I will have a least one healthy option to choose from on the menu. If I cannot choose the restaurant, I will review the menu online and make my selection ahead of time. Making the decision as to what I will eat before I arrive at the dinner helps me stay on track. I also pack my lunch for work every day. This pre-planning activity ensures I have a sufficient amount of food to curb my hunger during the day, which keeps me on track with my points and keeps me away from temptation when someone brings in some goodies to work.

Pre-planning is a key element to success in simplifying and de-stressing your life. It saves you time and allows you to make rational, unhurried choices in advance rather than making a quick decision in the heat of the moment. I have found I am more satisfied through pre-planning and have many fewer regrets about the decisions I made. Each of the three bee types, the worker bee, the (male) drone and the Queen Bee follow a prescribed activity plan. Pre-planning helps to alleviate some of the chaos in our lives. Please read on to learn some of the planning techniques I have used over the years to keep my personal life sane and orderly.

Pre-planning for the Holidays

Holidays can be our greatest joy and our biggest pain point. We enjoy coming together with our friends and family, sharing stories, exchanging presents and having some good old fashion fun. Yet the holidays can also serve as a point of frustration. We can feel rushed and anxious, fretting over gift purchases and food preparation, facing travel delays and navigating family issues. Having a plan will help ensure your holidays are filled with love, kindness and fun. Depending on how quirky your family is, you may need more of a battle plan, which makes planning even more important!

The holidays occur at the same time each year so you do have the opportunity to plan. For example, if you rotate the hosting of Thanksgiving each year, reach agreement during the current holiday celebration as to who will host the event the following year. Obtaining a commitment a year in advance allows you to think through the major activities for which you need to plan to ensure the holiday goes smoothly. If you have a child in college, you will want to make a mental note to book travel arrangements as soon as the school calendar is available. If you are contemplating home renovations, you will want to make sure you begin them in a timeframe that allows for a lot of cushion to ensure your house is not in disarray when you have guests.

I take the opportunity to create a high-level task list so I know the major tasks I need to tackle months in advance in order to achieve a successful outcome. If I decide I want to buy a fully prepared turkey, I note it so I can take advantage of coupons or sales from companies like HoneyBaked Ham or from catalogue retailers.

I have an older sister with special needs named Teresa who lives in a group home near Pittsburgh, PA. For the past several years, I have invited her to my home for Thanksgiving. During this time, we complete her Christmas shopping and she purchases and prepares her Christmas cards. When I drive my sister back home after the holiday, I also use this opportunity to deliver my Christmas presents to my fantastic little nieces and nephews.

This year the plans changed. My husband and I travelled over Thanksgiving, so my other sister Sue hosted Teresa for dinner. The fact that Teresa would not be visiting me over the Thanksgiving holiday did not relieve me of my duties to get her shopping done before the Christmas rush. Once I knew our time together would change, I created a plan for how I was going to fulfill my sister's needs to be prepared for the holidays. In this case, it required me moving the schedule forward; and completing all shopping (hers and mine) by the end of October. Once the target date was established, I could then take the necessary steps such as changing my work calendar and ordering presents for my nieces and nephews. With some organization, I was able to complete my shopping and help Teresa complete hers, all before October 31. With a little bit of planning, both Teresa and I were able to enjoy our holidays with family and loved ones.

Throughout the year, I keep a list of potential gift ideas, for others as well as myself, so I am not scrambling at the last minute. If I see something I like during the year and am confident the chance of return is low, I buy the item immediately. I also order as much online as possible so I don't have to fight the crowds. While I usually have the packages conveniently delivered to my door, if I am pressed for time, I will order multiple items from the same store for pick up so I am in and out quickly. When the packages arrive, I wrap a few each night in a spare room, which allows me to chip away at this time-consuming task, and I keep the door closed so I can leave all the trimmings out until I have completed my wrapping. I also buy my Christmas cards immediately after the holiday the prior year as a means to save money and provide the flexibility to complete my Christmas cards at any time I choose. This year, I completed these in October while binge watching *The Great British Baking Show*. I buy my wrapping paper on sale the prior year as well.

I realize you cannot buy everything immediately after the holiday and assure it will still be relevant for the next holiday. One year "Dora the Explorer" Valentine's Day cards are great, but the next year your child will have moved on to something else. Given that the retailers prepare for the holidays months ahead of time each year, you can use this vast timeline to complete one or two activities each week. Just prioritize which tasks to complete first. For example, you may not want to buy your school-age child his Halloween costume two months ahead of time because he may want to wait to see what his friends will choose so he can feel part of the group. On the other hand, if you are handing out treats, you can buy these items early because it is entirely your decision as to what you will give to the trick-or-treaters in the neighborhood.

School Activities

Most schools provide a calendar near the beginning of the school year. When my son was younger, I found it useful to review the calendar immediately and lock down key dates. Fall and spring breaks may require you to get childcare coverage or finalize vacation plans. The schedule of school related activities is also critical so you can coordinate transportation and ensure your child does not miss any practices or events. Creating a virtual family calendar helps keep everyone on track and lets you and your spouse or partner know whose turn it is to pick up your child. Obviously, things change during the year but getting a jump-start on the schedule gives you a little bit of wiggle room and helps you establish a routine.

Birthdays and Anniversaries

Birthdays and anniversaries take place on the same day every year, yet we often feel as if the day has snuck up on us. Set a reminder on your calendar for up to thirty days in advance so you can plan for a thoughtful gift and remember to purchase a card. The reminder allows me to make sure I have plenty of time to send the card or buy a gift. I always have a stack of cards on hand. I buy beautiful handcrafted blank cards and use them for birthdays, anniversaries, as sympathy or get-well cards and for celebratory events like the birth of a child or a promotion.

Annual Exams, Taxes and Other Dull Necessities

I try to schedule routine services around my birthday. One time I went too far and had my teeth cleaned, had a mammogram and OB/GYN exam all on the same day. Ouch! While I don't recommend having this many exams in one day, I do recommend clustering them around a specific time of year so you can ensure you remember to get these important procedures. Avoid having your children miss school or a practice, by scheduling their annual exams for the summer or on a school vacation day. Schedule these appointments as soon as you receive the school calendar so you won't have problems securing convenient dates and times.

Benjamin Franklin said, "Nothing is certain except for death and taxes." What is certain is that tax preparation is a pain in the butt! Tax preparation is always a challenge whether you are preparing your own or collecting the documentation to take to your accountant. A little bit of planning can help ease this process. While I am fortunate my husband handles our tax preparation, I do my part by setting up files to make it easier to pull all the necessary information together. After many years of working with this simple system, we have found it makes the preparation process a bit easier for him.

Pre-planning does not have to be an onerous process but it can significantly shorten your work effort and lower your stress level because you know you have the situation covered.

Preplanning your Vacation

The thought of preplanning your vacation sounds simple. You just have to ensure the kids are out of school and lock down the desired dates on the calendar. Not so fast. I find it difficult to schedule my vacation less than three months in advance, and even this amount of advance planning is inadequate at times. I have to navigate key events such as board and management team meetings. In addition, my calendar often fills up six months in advance for speaking engagements or conferences.

When my husband was also a busy executive, we often struggled to find mutually acceptable times for vacations. We have come to realize it is more conducive to our schedules to travel over the holidays because when fewer meetings are likely. When our son was still in school, Christmas Eve became our big celebration day and we headed to the airport on Christmas morning for vacation. Find your rhythm for vacations and schedule them as far in advance as possible. Quality time away from the office is critical to restoring your well-being.

Date Night

With our busy work and family schedules, we may struggle to take some adult time with our spouses or partners. I recall hearing the term "date night" for the first time twenty years ago. A man I worked with talked about the concept of going on a date with his wife every other week. I will admit, at the time, I laughed at the idea. I was spending a lot of time with my husband and we didn't feel the need to get dressed up and go out on a prescheduled date. In fact, our view was the opposite. We wanted to spend as much time with our son as possible because we knew he was going to grow up and leave the nest and we would never get that precious time back.

Now that our son has left home, my husband and I unofficially began having date nights because all the extracurricular activities that come along with having a child no longer existed. We called our trip to London over Thanksgiving "ten date nights" because we were able to enjoy all the grown up activities London has to offer such as theater, symphonies, museums and shopping.

How do you squeeze date night into an already tight schedule? Several options are available. You can take the same approach as my colleague and set a routine. Assume the first and third Wednesday of each month is date night. Schedule a sitter far in advance (then double check at least a week in advance to ensure the sitter is still available). You might choose to simplify the process by going to the exact same restaurant or you might rotate each time or be even more adventurous and find a different activity each time but be careful you're not overburdening yourself by having to come up with new and exciting ideas each time. The idea of date night is to simplify your life and enjoy each other's company.

You may consider another approach to date night and I refer to this one as the "filler" approach. With this method you find small pockets of time (refer to Chapter 11 for more). Looking back, I realize this is the approach my husband and I took. We would find small windows of time when our son was engaged in an activity we weren't required to attend and we would then do our own activity. We never did anything elaborate although we did go to New York once when he was at Summer Camp. Typically, we would grab a bite to eat, go for a walk or get some ice cream and just catch up with each other. We prefer simplicity so this approach of squeezing in a few moments here and there worked really well for us. I do believe date night to be important for busy couples and with a little preplanning; you can fit it into your very busy schedule.

Scheduling Time With Other Loved Ones

Besides your spouse or partner, you may want to spend alone time with your kids, parents, siblings or friends. Often these relationships can be the most challenging to keep together because of all your other duties. With a little bit of planning you can find some alone time with these loved ones.

After struggling with juggling career and family, one of my colleagues and her husband devised a plan that helped with the overload she was feeling. One night per week, her husband and their son spend time together. The two of them get quality bonding time and my colleague stays late at work that one evening catching up on her work so she can spend her weekends with her family without worrying about work.

If your parents live nearby invite them to come to your child's games or other events. They get the enjoyment of watching their grandchild play and can spend time catching up with you at the same time. My father-in-law is 88 years young and I rarely get to see him during the week. Instead, I carve out time on the weekends to visit with him. If the weather is nice, we take a walk or we hop in the car and get some ice cream and catch up on what is happening in our lives. In addition, I usually call him on my long commute home at the end of the week as a means to ensure we stay connected. In general, I use my commute time on the weekends or after hours to connect with my friends and family. I also use my travel to visit with friends. One of my friends lives in Nashville and I often visit this city for business. When I am in town, my friend and I have dinner, and on occasion, I will spend the weekend, which gives us time to hang out. A little preplanning allows me to ensure I stay connected with the people I care about the most.

"Every saint has a bee in his halo"

Elbert Hubbard

Chapter 5

Outsourcing

Companies that compete successfully in the marketplace must be effective and efficient. As a result, most major companies outsource pieces of or entire functions and processes to other companies in the United States and around the world. Few blink when a company manufactures clothing in China. Even fewer individuals refuse to buy services from companies who outsource their relationships with customers by having calls handled in India or the Philippines. But if a parent sends his or her child to school with a store bought snack, even a healthy one, there's a good chance she'll be criticized (and it is usually the mother who gets criticized) for not prioritizing the needs of her family over her work. None of us wants to disappoint our family so we have a tendency to over compensate. We attempt to make the handmade costume for the Halloween parade or whip up a gluten-free, sugar-free snack on a moment's notice for the kindergarten class and inevitably, we sacrifice something else that is likely more important. Let's face it, most times the costume looks terrible or the snack tastes like cardboard and we are both embarrassed and guilt ridden. We also suffer for the next few days due to lack of sleep or because we've missed a deadline at work, simply because we tried to be superwoman.

By segregating the daily tasks required to keep the colony alive, even bees are engaged in outsourcing of sorts. For example, male drones only serve one purpose – to mate. (I am not joking)! They leave the other tasks to the worker bees (all of whom happen to be female - no comment)! The worker bees divide their tasks too! Not even real worker bees attempt to do it all, and neither should you.

We can use two well-known business concepts to illustrate how we determine where to focus our time and attention. The first concept, "Return on Investment" (ROI), or "Return on Invested Capital" (ROIC), refers to an evaluation as to where to allocate a company's precious assets (human and capital) as a means in bringing an organization the greatest returns (profits). A company may have to choose between investing its cash in a new market expansion or in investing that same cash in technology enhancements. In conducting this assessment, the company looks at the costs and benefits of each project over a designated time period and then, the company typically funds the project, which produces the best financial return or best positions the company for the long term.

We can translate this concept into our personal lives. Choosing between entering the workforce immediately after high school rather than investing in a college education can be an example of making a decision based on return on investment. Often (but not always) an individual who chooses to forgo additional education and immediately joins the workforce will find herself earning more money initially than she would earn if she were attending college during that same time period. However, over time, her earnings will typically be less than if she attended college because many college graduates have opportunities to earn higher income due to making that investment early on.

In other words, by taking a longer-term view, and investing your human (time) and capital (money) resources in a good college education early on, your income (i.e., profits) will be greater over your lifetime. The ROIC concept applies to other choices in our personal lives as well. You may choose to invest in a cleaning professional so you can take a course to further your passion, thereby earning more income, which more than offsets the cost of the cleaning assistance. You may choose to forgo your daily Starbucks habit and instead invest those dollars in paying for dues to a society or club for professionals like yourself (i.e., engineers, actuaries, human resource professionals). While the satisfaction in sipping your Grande mocha latte is immediate, if you regularly attend and network at these society meetings you will be much more likely to profit from the relationships you will form.

While the ROIC typically looks at a longer time period, you should use this concept to make some short-term decisions as well. Should I spend five hours making little Ian's Halloween costume (a trip to the store to purchase the materials and then the time to actually make the outfit) or should I invest those precious hours into another activity such as spending time *playing* with Ian? No brainer! Should I volunteer to do an extra activity on Saturday morning or do I sleep in for an extra hour. Some might think my suggestion to skip a volunteer activity is selfish and that may be the case. What's most important is for you to choose which activities you want to continue and those you want to stop. Remember, the Queen Bee focused her energy on herself so she could do her job well and you need to focus your efforts as well so you can become the type of Queen Bee you choose.

Another concept in business is focusing on the core, which means an organization should determine which core capabilities, activities and investments are critical to it being successful in its main business. Once the organization determines its core capabilities, it can then begin to make decisions whether to outsource non-core capabilities or stop offering certain products or services. Imagine you are an owner of a company that makes delicious chocolate chip cookies, which would be my dream job! Of course, you want the freshest and best ingredients because they are core to the cookie's taste. You carefully select the suppliers for the eggs, flour, sugar and chocolate. You may decide the freshness of the eggs matters so much that you choose to own and operate a nearby chicken farm. On the other hand, maybe you own a cocoa bean farm. You also know brand and packaging are an important part of the consumer experience so you ensure the packaging is appealing and of good quality so the cookies don't crumble during the process of shipping. Shipping on the other hand is not a differentiator because you have determined the large shipping companies are equally reliable. You purchase this delivery service based on price and you don't try to start a transportation company because shipping is not a core capability of your company. Your customers don't know and don't care how their favorite chocolate chip cookies arrived at the grocery store. All they care about is that the cookies are available in their local store when they want them and they come in a nice looking container that keeps the cookies fresh and intact.

Apply this concept of focusing on the core to your personal life. Your family needs to eat but do they really care if you make the dinner or if someone else makes it and you reheat it? Do your kids ever ask who washes their jeans? Likely, they just care that their favorite pair is clean and in their drawer. In this chapter, I hope you will find the push you need to consider outsourcing what might appear to be even the most trivial of activities and I urge you to think very hard about saying yes to many of these suggestions.

As I think about ROIC or focusing on the core, the question I am really asking is whether an activity or task is meaningful enough to require my limited time and attention. I ask myself, "Am I receiving something *meaningful* in return when I undertake a project outside the office?" In other words, do I get "Return on Meaning?" (ROM).

When I do take the time to plant a few flowers or to walk around my back yard and pick up some sticks, (a carryover from my Girl Scout days foraging in the forest for kindling wood) is there a ROM? When I undertake either of these activities, I most definitely get a ROM! I usually wander out into the yard or get the urge to plant some flowers because I need a mental break from work. I need an activity that gets me outdoors into the fresh air and sunshine and allows me to complete a small task very quickly. The sense of accomplishment coupled with the brief change of scenery helps me clear my head so I can return ready to focus on my work with a renewed focus.

As you read the remainder of this chapter on outsourcing, you might be confused because I suggest you outsource major activities like planting flowers and yard work, yet I just shared an example of me undertaking these very tasks. The activities I just referenced are examples of providing myself a small *respite* as I complete the activity within a short time period and do not engage in ongoing maintenance. *I choose* to outsource the heavy lifting and to take on smaller tasks only when I feel like it. By the way, sometimes my idea of planting consists of purchasing a hanging basket, cutting off the wires and plopping it into the planter. I have been doing this for years and my neighbors can't get over what a green thumb I have! Please do read on for many more tips on when to outsource.

One of the first questions I ask an individual who says she want to climb the corporate ladder is whether she uses a cleaning professional. (I use the term professional because these individuals have my complete admiration. In addition, there are men who actually do house cleaning for hire). At least fifty percent of the time the response I receive is "no," and half of these responses include a statement such as "I enjoy cleaning," and "it takes my mind off of work." Let's just say for the sake of argument that you do enjoy sticking your hand down a toilet bowl. The point is not whether you enjoy cleaning. I like getting rid of stuff and hauling it to the Goodwill. Rather, the point is whether you can do something more worthy of your time or more meaningful with the extra time you have when you are not cleaning. Cleaning is an activity requiring too much time and effort. Cleaning is a necessity for sure. It is also a basic activity not requiring your specific skills and, therefore; should be outsourced. Even if you are a stickler for a clean house and frugal when it comes to parting with money, hiring a cleaning professional is one of the best decisions you can make. If the idea of having someone come into your home feels odd to you, consider outsourcing in baby steps. Have the cleaning professional start with cleaning the bathroom and kitchen only and then upgrade from there.

When is the last time you said to yourself, "I remember the time I really cleaned the bathroom and it sparkled!" I will bet you have never said that. When has your spouse said, "The thing I appreciate/love about you the most is your ability to clean." May a party guest compliments you on the cleanliness of your home? What? Never? Hmmm . . . this might be a clue that spending your time cleaning does not matter to anyone, and it can and should be outsourced.

Please take note: whomever you choose to clean your home will not clean the way you do. This individual will have his or her own system. The placement of items will not be the way you like but you will need to get over it. You will hear more about not redoing someone else's work in Chapter 10, I'm Perfect . . . You're not.

Many people believe they cannot afford to hire someone to clean their homes. I challenge this idea. Step back and think about where you are spending your money and not maximizing the value you receive in return. Are you buying a mocha latte at Starbucks a few times a week? At $3.00 per cup five days a week that's or $60 per month or $720 per year! This amount will surely help cover a good portion of the cost for a cleaning professional. How much are you spending on the extra channels you buy from your cable or satellite TV provider? You can easily pay $150 or more per month and not use many of the services. Consider downsizing to a smaller bundle of services or switch to another less expensive content provider as a means to fund the services of a cleaning professional. If your family balks, help them to understand what's in it for them (i.e., more time with Mom or Dad), although this pitch does *not* work on teenagers who may have no desire to spend more time with you!

As an alternative to paying for professional services, require your kids to do some light housework. At a minimum, have them clean their own rooms really well each week and wash their own sheets and laundry. These minor activities teach them skills they will need as adults and help them become responsible. If you are asking your kids to take on additional cleaning for areas that the entire family uses, pay them if you can or make their allowance dependent on these small cleaning duties. You will get a cleaner house and they will have a little pocket money.

I urge people to consider paying for a cleaning professional as an investment in their careers. I have shared with individuals on many occasions that they will be earning back the amount of money they are spending on cleaning services and will likely be earning even more than that within two years. No one has ever told me hiring a cleaning professional was a bad decision. Whether these individuals earned more or just had more time to do the things they really wanted, people who outsource cleaning consistently believe it is a good investment.

One day while visiting one of our sales offices I had the opportunity to spend some time with a small group of the younger professionals in the office. They asked me to share some tips and, of course, I immediately guided them toward outsourcing their cleaning to a professional. A few months later I was attending an event for the top sales people in our organization and a woman approached me, gave me a big hug and said "I really want to thank you!" I had never seen this woman before so I was anxious to hear what I had done to deserve that hug and her appreciation. She told me her husband was in the group of young professionals with whom I had spoken months earlier and when he arrived home that evening he announced they were going to hire someone to do their cleaning. This statement was music to her ears.

The husband then approached us and shared his own epiphany. He realized if he stayed in the office one extra hour each week, he could probably make enough additional phone calls that would result in at least one additional sale per month, which would also cover the cost of a lawn service. He would also reduce his commute time by avoiding rush hour traffic. I was pleased this young man took the outsourcing initiative one-step further. Sure enough, he was able to close enough additional cases routinely to cover the cost of both the cleaning and lawn services and then some. As evidenced by his attendance at the sales event for the top 20 percent highest achieving sales executives, I would say his investment in outsourcing earned him a great return both financially and with his family.

Cooking and baking are two other activities that can easily be outsourced. While I happen to enjoy both of these activities, many people do not have either the time or the interest in the culinary arts. Many companies now deliver nutritious ingredients to your kitchen for you to prepare delicious meals. Most of these services allow you to skip grocery shopping and limit the food preparation to get dinner quickly on the table. Other services provide the ingredients but the prep time is still too long. Do your investigative homework and choose wisely. If your budget allows, you can find someone who will prepare all the meals in advance and you simply heat and serve. Grocery stores now have reasonable "grab and go" prepackaged meals as an option. Any one of these approaches ensures that your family is eating well and not over-indulging in calories. Remember to consider trade-offs if cost is a concern.

If these options seem too complicated or too expensive, with a little planning you can determine a budget friendly plan that works for you. Make a list of healthy foods that are either ready to go or can be prepared quickly, stock up on these items and mix and match for a fast, healthy meal. Examples include yogurt, eggs, diced chicken breast, cheese, soup, low calorie or whole-wheat pasta, and on and on. I have a list of standard food items in my refrigerator and pantry so I can always grab a quick healthy meal when I am tired or rushed. I find that having these "go to" items helps me make healthy choices and maintain my weight. Also, watch for healthy frozen meals to go on sale too. With a little creativity, you can find plenty of opportunities to enjoy a quick, healthy meal.

Make a list of activities that do not have meaning in your life but *must* be done such as cleaning, lawn care, dishes, cooking, shopping, etc., and prioritize them based on the amount of precious time they take away from more meaningful activities or choose based on what you dislike doing the most. If you absolutely hate to run errands or go to the grocery store then move these activities to the top of the outsourcing list. The Appendix contains a list of routine activities to outsource.

Critical and Meaningful Tasks

Sometimes we have to outsource tasks that are meaningful because these tasks are not our core competency. Many household maintenance activities fall into this category. My husband and I would never attempt to cut down a large tree as we lack the competency to tackle such an activity. Maybe the activity involves helping a loved one and the task is beyond your reach. If this is the case, it is even more critical to outsource. If your daughter is struggling with trigonometry and, (like me) you don't have a clue how to help her, outsource this job to a professional so she can get the assistance she needs and deserves. A friend of mine's daughter was ill when she was younger and as a result fell behind in school. The mother was a single, hard-working professional who was smart, but did not feel she could really give her child the instruction she needed to get back on track. The mother hired a tutor to help her daughter get back on track in reading and math so she could perform on the same level as her fellow classmates. Within several months, her daughter was back on track and today she is an actuary at a major insurance company. If your son has some talent as a tuba player or your daughter is skilled at golf you wouldn't hesitate to hire an expert to assist them in learning the critical skills to put them on a path to success. Outsource a meaningful is acceptable when you know it is the way to get the best outcome.

Caregiving is an extremely personal matter and I don't take it lightly by including it in this chapter on outsourcing. Caregiving takes a variety of forms from managing finances and navigating the healthcare system to helping with activities of daily living. I have plenty of experience in caregiving with both elderly and special needs family members, and often it has involved traveling long distances regularly, which further complicates matters. Even though I shared the caregiving duties for my mother and sister, Teresa, with my other sister, Sue, and my nephew, Butch, the entire process was exhausting. Between trying to keep track of whose turn it was to visit the house, determining whether my mother had taken her medication or ensuring my sister Teresa had her lunch packed for work, all three of us were anxious fearing we missed something.

Don't go it alone as a caregiver. Seek as much assistance as possible from others as a means to minimize your time commitment. That might sound harsh, but as I suspect many of you know, unexpected situations arise constantly with loved ones who need special care, so your weekly time commitment will usually be greater than anticipated.

In our family, we split the effort based on our own skills. I served as the chief financial officer paying the bills, obtaining the powers of attorney and wills and navigating the health care system. I was the one tasked with choosing the best health plan coverage, scheduling my mother and sister's doctor visits scheduled and arranging transportation and ensuring their medications arrived at the front door like clockwork. My sister, Sue, was the on-the-ground supervisor. She visited the home regularly, stocked the pantry with groceries, tossed expired food from the refrigerator, did the laundry and verified medication consumption. My nephew, Butch, was the handy man. He cut the grass each week, made household repairs and ensured the furnace and other major appliances were in good working order. Dividing the duties based on each of our skills allowed us to leverage our strengths and work more efficiently as a team.

We got to the point where in-home care became a necessity and eventually assisted living was required. While you will always feel guilty having to invade a loved one's privacy in their home or worse, moving them to another living arrangement, deciding as a team helps to relieve some of that guilt. We determined the safety of my mother and sister was paramount and trumped any dislike by my mother for assisted care. When my mother had to move to an assisted living facility, my special needs sister moved to a group home. Imagine the guilt I felt after removing mother from the home she built and my sister from her home where she had lived with her parents for more than half of her life! We soon discovered that everyone adjusts, and my sister, Teresa, adapted to her new living arrangement like a duck to water. She is thriving in her new home. She is now able to enjoy shopping and eating out with her friends, bowling or going to a movie. She has also taken several vacations, something not possible under her prior living arrangement.

Caregiving is the hardest thing you will ever do in your life, and it takes a toll on your emotional and physical wellbeing. My stress levels and weight soared in the wrong direction during the last two years my mother was alive. I encourage you not to allow the guilt overtake your good judgment. If you can afford to outsource most or even a little of the care to a home health professional, then do so. Trust me, you will remain actively involved in their care and you will still worry but the in-home help will be a lifeline. If you cannot afford to pay someone, then tap into *all* your family members including brothers, sisters, spouses, children and grandchildren, as well as friends and neighbors to help you manage the situation. Make a commitment to assist them when they have a similar caregiving need.

Explore public sources to help you fill in the gaps. I have found a way to utilize these resources to benefit my sister and lighten my load. For example, I would routinely drive seven hours round trip to take her shopping for the day. Recently, she wanted to attend a summer camp. I was able to take care of all the paper work online, but she needed to buy some basics for camp. My work schedule was causing me to travel more than usual, making it difficult for me to find the time to take her shopping. I shared my predicament with several of my friends at one of our evening gatherings. One of them suggested that I ask one of the staff to meet me half way. I thought that was a brilliant idea, and one for which I was willing to pay. When I asked the staff supervisor, she informed me that transportation for my sister to see her family was a covered service. Because I was able to meet them half way, I had extra time to spend with my sister. A win/win for sure!

Outsourcing the Holidays

I am not advocating a repeat of the movie *Christmas with the Kranks*, but I am suggesting that navigating the holidays can be one of your biggest challenges. Holidays are supposed to be joyful, but getting to the big day can prove to be very stressful. We set high expectations for these special times in our lives and as a result, we overextend ourselves. Once I decided to create an "old fashioned" holiday and talked myself into preparing the entire meal from scratch. In my mind, this meant I needed to brine the turkey, which I had never before attempted. I was clueless about the entire process. Since it was my first time, I had to buy a special container large enough to let the bird soak overnight. I made a special trip to the local Home Depot to find a plastic container large enough to hold the big bird. Next, I realized I had to reposition *everything* in my refrigerator, which involved pulling out shelves, tossing out food and very carefully balancing the remaining items on top of the now full Home Depot container. Not simply satisfied with just roasting the turkey, I decided the pies, mashed potatoes and rolls should also be homemade. By the time dinner was over, I was exhausted. Was it worth it? Absolutely not! My family cared more about getting back to watching the football games on TV than they did about my fancy cooking and baking. While everyone else was having fun I was in the kitchen cooking and then cleaning up. Holidays are supposed to be about spending time with your family. However, year after year I hear people talk about how tired they are when they return to work. The bottom line is that holiday meals present the perfect opportunity for outsourcing.

Many restaurants offer the option of pre-ordering a dinner with all the trimmings. You need only to pick up the food, reheat a few items and your meal is ready to go. I have fully outsourced my holiday meals on several occasions and yes, I have had a few mishaps here and there. In Ohio, a local restaurant chain advertises fully cooked holiday meals. I had ordered from this restaurant in the past without issue. One year the local store employed a manager who, unfortunately, was not on top of her game. After waiting impatiently for over an hour my husband texted me and stated he was not waiting any longer for our order. I persuaded him to wait because I did not have a plan and my in-laws were in town visiting. He arrived home an hour later with a complete meal and a surly attitude, but Thanksgiving was saved. We later learned the restaurant ran out of turkey that day! I have ordered since without incident, but now I also have a backup, just in case things do not go as planned.

When I have been willing to tackle a little more food preparation for a big holiday meal, I shift from home made to home heated (or microwaved). I usually purchase pre-cooked meat (i.e., turkey breast or ham), microwavable side dishes and fully baked delicious pies from my favorite bakery. The only "baking" I do is to pop my favorite Pillsbury dinner rolls into the oven. Are these options more expensive than making a meal from scratch? Maybe, if you look exclusively at the cost in terms of dollars, but I put a price on my time and my sanity, and by factoring these two elements into the equation, I think it's well worth the cost. As I mentioned before, I love to bake and cook. Any of my family, friends or work colleagues can share countless stories of eating one of my baked delights (yes, I am a good baker which was another reason I struggled with my weight). I *choose* to bake when I want to relax or need an activity. I no longer bake because it is a holiday or because someone else expects it. I bake on my terms and on my timing. Cooking and baking serve to restore my wellbeing. Because I outsourced the main meal this most recent Christmas holiday, I chose to make Quiche Lorraine for my family for breakfast. We all enjoyed this treat and I did not feel overwhelmed at the thought of making this one simple meal.

Some other thoughts on the holidays.

As I write this, my husband and have returned from a trip to London over Thanksgiving. This year, my Thanksgiving (and birthday) dinner consisted of a ham and cheese baguette at a musical venue where we watched the BBC Symphony Orchestra. Enjoying that sandwich with my husband just before the show reinforced our decision to forgo the traditional celebrations. Spending some time together was the right decision for us and for that, I am extremely thankful.

Planning. As I mentioned in Chapter 4, take a few minutes and jot down a plan for the holiday. Think of everything you want to accomplish, then review your plan again and eliminate half of your items. This approach requires to you prioritize what is really important and then allows you to focus all of your attention on meaningful activities that really matter and that you want to get right.

Hosting holiday events. Answer this question. Why are you hosting anything? What is your real motivation for hosting? Maybe you are making it easier on yourself having everyone come to your home instead of packing your kids and the dog into the car and driving to Grandma's or your sister's home. Perhaps you are unwilling to relinquish control to someone else because you are afraid your perfect holiday will fail to materialize. Maybe others have simply taken advantage of your generosity, or have designated you as the host because your house is a little bit bigger. Ensure you have an understanding and are in complete acceptance of why you are the host; otherwise, it is time to rotate the honor to another family member.

Traditions can morph over time. You don't have to follow the exact same routine every single year. For example, many families rotate the hosting responsibilities each year. If you have been hosting the same event year over year (except maybe your child's birthday), shake it up a little. Encourage others to take their turn. If you must be the host, then use a catering or takeout service. This approach might cost a little more (remember you can cut back on other activities to fund your outsourcing), but you will be able to more fully experience and enjoy your gathering. Moreover, remember to have your house professionally cleaned before the big event!

Have everyone play a role. If you are like me, you're good at recruiting people to assist you at work. Take the same approach for your holiday event. Most people want to help, so simply ask them to bring a side dish, dessert or a beverage. If you feel uncomfortable asking individuals in person to assist, simply note on the invitation you would appreciate each attendee contributing to the meal. While I cannot recall the exact wording, I remember receiving a creative invitation with a request worded something like this:

> *Let's celebrate the holidays together! I'll buy the wine, (maybe something stronger), and you bring the cheese, crackers, chocolates, ice cream or whatever simple goodies you like so we can focus on catching up and having fun!*

What I love about this invitation is the thought and intention of the host. She made it clear the evening was about being together and gave her guests permission to bring the easiest food as possible.

If you receive an invitation to a party and with a request to bring a *specific* dish, decline the invitation! I am not referring to a request for a simple side dish or salad. Allow me to explain. Shortly after my husband and I were married, we received an invitation to attend a dinner club. We were new to the community and I thought it might be a good way to meet the neighbors. The invitation included a request to bring a side dish, and over the next few days as I was pondering what to make, a recipe appeared in my mailbox. I was curious as to why a specific recipe was required, so naively I asked a neighbor. She kindly informed me that the members of the club wanted to ensure the food contributions were 'suitable,' fearing that without a prepared recipe some of the participants might resort to bringing something mundane like "Jell-O with fruit and Cool Whip." This conversation was the first red flag and had I been smart enough, I would have cancelled out of the event on the spot.

I prepared a list of the ingredients needed to to make this "suitable" side dish (which included rice and I don't even care for rice). As I was leaving for the store, I received a phone call asking me to substitute pecans for the walnuts in the recipe. Red flag number two. I made the mental note to purchase pecans in lieu of walnuts and asked the caller if the event was casual. She sounded horrified that I even posed this question. Blue jeans were definitely not acceptable. I bit my tongue. Red flag number three.

The following Saturday I made the horrid rice dish (pecans, no walnuts), put on a nice sweater and pair of slacks and walked about thirty yards to my neighbor's house. Although everyone was nice enough, my husband and I found that we did not enjoy the company enough to continue with these outings. We decided to decline future invitations including those that extended beyond the dinner club to block parties and other neighborhood events. You might consider us a full of ourselves for not joining in the neighborhood merriment, but in our view, we were simply making the choice to spend more time together as a couple and a family. Looking back, I am confident we made the right decision.

I share this story to demonstrate that while my initial reason for joining the dinner club was reasonable (i.e., to meet new people), I failed to think through how such a commitment might steal my precious time. The food preparation alone required a significant amount of investment. Instead, I should have been devoting that time to my family and myself. Furthermore, a dinner club means many, many weekend dinners.

I have learned over the years how to avoid immediately committing when presented with a verbal invitation. Verbal invitations catch me off guard so they can be the most difficult to decline. I have learned to respond by saying, "I'll get back to you." If someone presses me to see if I have another commitment, I simply repeat the phrase again. The individual extending the invitation quickly gets the message that I will lock myself into an immediate acceptance. Another simple response is, "I've got plans." You do not have to disclose what these plans are, nor do you have to feel guilty if your plan is to lay on the couch and watch television. In the spirit of pre-planning, have your 'go-to' statement ready to buy yourself time to clearly think through your response and avoid committing yourself to an activity that is not of interest.

Cookie Exchanges. Beware of the cookie exchange – it's a trap! You think you are being smart because you make a few dozen of one type of cookie and get dozens of cookies in return. Then you discover the cookie exchange has rules, which excludes all the basic, easy recipes and requires you to make cookies that require significant time and effort. Participants must demonstrate their superior baking skills by making delicacies such as Russian teacakes, lady locks or springerle, which take hours to bake.

One year I decided to make gobs, which are a sandwich-type cookie with frosting in the middle. If you grew up near Pittsburgh, Pennsylvania, you will totally understand my reference. Do the math. You can see I was a fool to make these cookies! To get the twenty dozen cookies needed for the exchange I had to make forty dozen, and then spend time icing and assembling them. The other participants were very disappointed when I declined to participate the following year because my gobs are delicious and no one else makes them, but I held firm.

Beyond the cookie exchange, banish the idea of any homemade gift for the holidays. I used to make pounds and pounds of chocolate candies and distribute them to co-workers, friends and family around the country. While I loved to hear how yummy my creations were, clearly the recipients would have been just as happy if I handed out some store-bought chocolates or if I had taken the same amount of time and provided a heartfelt written note of thanks for their hard work, kindness, friendship, etc. After all, being thankful is the key message of our holidays. I must confess I clung to my candy making for many, many years but I eventually came to my senses and finally stopped the practice a few years ago. I am living a healthier lifestyle and I suspect no one really misses my candies.

Because I do love to make treats, I now periodically bake for my work colleagues, but again, it is on my terms. If you feel like you want to provide baked foods as presents or want to ensure your family has plenty of goodies over the holidays, then find a local bakery and place your order.

Gifts and wrapping. I must confess I love wrapping gifts and go to great pains to make them look beautiful. I wrap the gifts as I buy them so I am not overwhelmed at the last minute. I know gift-wrapping is not something most people enjoy, and this activity is ripe for outsourcing. Most online purchases have a gift-wrap option for a small fee. Many of the major stores also have gift-wrapping available or allow a local non-profit organization to raise funds this way. If the thought of paying a gift-wrapping fee is intolerable, then go with the tried and true gift bag and tissue paper. Nothing is easier and the bags always look great.

You can simplify your shopping as well by buying in bulk. For years, I bought every team member the same item. One year I bought them beautiful wreaths from Lynch Creek Farms in the Pacific Northwest. Another year I bought the team bread from Zingerman's Deli. If I cannot decide on the gift, then I buy gift cards. Now, my team and I forego the gift exchange. Instead, we all chip in to buy gifts for a needy family. We go shopping, then wrap the gifts together and have a team dinner. Our time together is fun, simple and much more meaningful and charitable.

Prepare yourself for unexpected gifts. I have been the recipient of an impromptu gift. In the past, I have immediately felt the need to reciprocate. If you feel that need, have a few extra small gifts on hand to give. If you do not feel the need to return the gesture, then you can give those gifts to someone else who has helped you out throughout the year, works extra hard, or maybe is just having a difficult time. Handmade soaps and candies are always a good fallback. What you don't give away, you can use yourself.

Obviously, you have to put more thought into gifts for your family. I try to take note of items my friends and family mention throughout the year so I am prepared when the time comes to purchase the gift. For my little nieces and nephews I check out the list of the hot items and request input from the kids themselves. I am not embarrassed to ask the recipient if there is something specific they really want. I do the vast majority of my research and purchasing online.

Although I always have the holiday spirit, I can feel overwhelmed with the idea of purchasing many gifts. Years ago, I found myself exchanging gifts with several dear work colleagues. I had only known these individuals for a few years and I felt pressure to ensure that I was buying them beautiful gifts. The pressure was purely internal, but nonetheless it was real to me. These women were sophisticated and worldly and could purchase many beautiful things. I didn't feel I could do them justice without going overboard. Finally, after a few years I shared with each one independently that I preferred to stop the purchases and instead would rather enjoy their company for an evening at dinner. We changed our routine and if any one of them were disappointed in my decision, they never let their feelings show.

Recently I was staying at my best friend's home in Pittsburgh. I always say it is the best hotel in the city, a clean room, delicious food and great company. During this trip I was sharing with her how I had to get all my Christmas shopping for my sisters, nieces and nephews completed earlier than usual, and I still had more shopping to do for my immediate family and others. To my surprise she said, "We don't have to exchange Christmas gifts. It will be one less thing on our lists." I was surprised since my friend is an ardent and generous gift giver. She sends gifts year round for small celebrations and as a thank you. Of course, I quickly agreed with her suggestion and pushed even further suggesting to my friend that we not exchange birthday gifts either, but she drew the line at Christmas, which I agreed with – for now!

Holiday Decorating. Decorating can be one of the most challenging aspects of the holidays. I used to spend two full days putting up lights outside my home. Now I put a wreath (usually purchased online and delivered to my home) on the door with a single spotlight. Electric candles adorn each window and that is it. In my mind simple equals elegance. The house looks just as much if not more beautiful than when I used to install outdoor lights. If you feel the need for extensive outdoor decorations, keep it to a minimum. A colleague suggests using laser lights on the outside of the house to keep things simple or perhaps you should hire a company to handle this chore for you. You will have to schedule the service far in advance and it will cost you, but you may decide it is worth it. The beauty of outsourcing is that *you* get to decide how your hard-earned money is spent. I used a service one year and was not pleased with either their decorating or clean up skills. After that experience, I stopped the extensive outdoor decorations and I have never looked back.

As for the inside of the house, keep it simple. If you have young children you will likely want to have a tree, religious artifacts or other decorations depending on the holiday. Step back and think about what is important to make your house special for the holidays. More is not necessarily better. A few years, I put lights and fake snow on my tree and that was all. At night, it looked beautiful, during the day not so much, but it worked for us. Several years, including this most recent year, I have skipped the tree. Setting up and decorating the tree is very time consuming and I simply didn't have enough time to commit to this activity without something more important falling to the wayside. Dismantling the tree also requires quite a bit of work. I have also been in the position where my decorated artificial tree stood proudly in the front window until about March and it drove my neighbor across the street mad! While I would have enjoyed having a tree, I know I made the right decision this year to forgo this activity. Maybe next year I will have a tree.

A friend shared a great holiday tree tradition with me. Having a decorated tree is important to their family. Her husband buys the tree and my friend and her daughters do the decorating. In addition, each year she challenges her spouse to find the smallest full-sized tree possible which makes it easier to decorate the tree. Another option is to have a tabletop tree or multiple tabletop trees throughout the house. This approach becomes even easier when your children are grown and leave the house.

Do not let people judge you or coerce you into decorating. In years past when I chose not to set up a tree, I would volunteer this information as I joined in discussions with others about how effort is required to prepare for the holidays. I could always count on at least one person using guilt tactics to get me to change my mind. Little do they know this only serves to have me further dig in my heels. I heard comments such as, "Your son is traveling hundreds of miles to see you and you won't even have a tree for him?" My son is an adult and he is fine without a tree. If you really want to know whether your family wants all these decorations, tell them they are responsible for putting specific decorations up and taking them down. Instruct them specifically as to which days the décor will go up and which days the décor must come down. Then inform them you will be blocking everyone's calendars so they all participate – no exceptions. My guess is you will see quickly most of your family members really don't care about the décor; they really just want to hang out and have fun! Try it and see for yourself. If they are willing to make the commitment to decorate and put everything away afterwards, then decorate until your heart is content!

If decorating is important to you, think about hosting a decorating party with your friends. I suggest serving plenty of food and drink prepared by someone else. The outcome might not be exactly as planned but you will have a lot of fun in the process. Don't forget you can hire someone to decorate the inside of your home as well as the outside (and you can tell the kids that Santa, or a wicked witch did the decorating).

Retail marketing has convinced us that we have to decorate for every holiday in the year. My sister Teresa for example, decorates her room and the entire group home for every holiday including Valentine's Day, St. Patrick's Day and the Fourth of July. We do have excessive holiday decorating within our family DNA. I have managed to suppress this gene. I decorate extensively for Christmas and in the fall; I switch up a few pillow covers and retrieve a few glass pumpkins from the basement. If you have the holiday decorating bug then consider cutting back. You do not have to create an extravaganza for every holiday. Choose one or two holidays in which you will invest your decorating skills and time. If you have small children you'll likely feel the need to do some decorating, but do not feel the need to go all out for every holiday. If you celebrate Easter, color some eggs as a family and set the kid's baskets around the house for decoration. Keep it simple and easy!

Decorating for Halloween seems to be as intense as decorating for Christmas. Scale it back by purchasing a few pumpkins, some stencils and paint, and let your kids hone their artistic skills. Unless your kid is a carving genius and is vying to win a full college pumpkin carving scholarship, stay away from the pumpkin carving. The process is just too messy and not worth the effort. Whichever holidays you choose to test your decorating abilities, think simple or outsource and keep your stress levels low.

Card etiquette in the modern world. Standard convention may tell us we must reciprocate for every card we receive, but I chose to ignore the standards. I send cards (birthday or holiday) to those people I truly want to stay in touch with and to work colleagues. For those dear to me, I write a personal note sharing how I am doing and inquire the same. A typed letter is also acceptable because the whole point of the communication is to share what has been happening in your life the previous year. While I have never typed a letter, although I think update letters have merit, I have received numerous comments over the years as to how people enjoy reading my handwritten updates. The people you send cards to care about you and want to read about your life's adventures. So write away, but only to those people with whom you really have a connection, otherwise point them to your

Facebook page. I keep the card from the prior year so I can refresh my memory as to the information the sender shared and so I can readily obtain their home address from the envelope. Those who fail to include a return address may risk deletion from the mailing list. When I finish writing out the new cards the old ones go into the trash. This system saves me time from having to update my address book. If I were using printed labels it would make sense for me to retain the information online, but my limited stack of cards is very manageable.

Note that I separated out my work colleagues because I feel an obligation to send them a card. (Sorry folks that is just the way it is). I don't take time to share any personal information with my work colleagues, rather, I simply wish them a happy holiday and sign my name. Maybe I will become braver and just take them off my list someday.

Years ago, I made drastic cuts on my card list and here is how I took that step. Firstly, I stopped sending cards to anyone who has not sent me a card in the prior two years. Secondly, I realized that anyone who simply signs their name and has no news to share (work colleagues are the exception here) was more of an acquaintance than a true friend so I deleted them from the list. I applied the same lens to those whose card I continuously receive after the holidays. These people were simply signing their names and obviously had a lot on their plates. I could help lighten their burden by removing them from the list. Finally,

I deleted those individuals whose connections to me had been tenuous at best and were now broken (e.g., a former work colleague). I just completed this same analysis for my most recent round of holiday cards and deleted about a dozen names from the list, which freed up time for me to write some more meaningful notes to friends. My advice is to stop feeling guilty about not responding to every card and enjoy an activity with your family.

Funding your outsourcing activities

As I mentioned earlier, the biggest challenge most people face with outsourcing is finding the money to pay for these services. People often view outsourcing exclusively as an added cost and therefore believe they cannot afford to outsource an activity. In truth, you cannot afford not to outsource but it takes some thought and – you guessed it – planning.

Since outsourcing is not free, you must reconfigure your household expenditures to cover the cost. Prioritize your outsourcing by listing those activities that consume most of your time and bring you the least Return on Meaning (ROM), then slowly outsource more activities as you recover income from stopping other activities or as your income increases. How do you find the money to outsource, especially when most of us already have a tight budget? Start by looking at where you are spending your money today and reroute those funds currently paying for non-essentials to pay for necessary activities that consume your precious time or cause you a great deal of stress. For example, stop the morning drive through coffee habit and make coffee at home or wait and drink the free coffee at the office. If you really enjoy the fancy flavors you get at a coffee shop, buy an enhancer such as vanilla almond milk and it will feel as if you are having a treat. You can easily save $60 a month, and use that money to have someone clean your house, mow the lawn or wash your windows. Take the bus instead of driving to work. Some companies subsidize bus fare. You will save on gas, parking and wear and tear on your car. You can also lower your car insurance fees since you are driving fewer miles and you can use the bus time to read, or catch up on email, podcasts or other activities. One of my friends uses her evening bus trip home to call her mother. She simply puts on her headphones, mutes the background noise and lets her mother talk until her heart is content. The defined timeframe of the bus ride ensures that the conversation does not spill over into her time with her kids and husband and, in the process, she feels like she is being a good daughter.

Downsize your cable or satellite package or cut the cord completely and choose a lower cost video streaming service. Another friend of mine regularly renegotiated her cable bill downward every few months until she finally cut the cord. Record free television shows or movies so you will always have something to watch on a rainy day. You will discover that without the TV luring you into the family room each night, you will accomplish more at home, your family will stay more connected and you'll feel more relaxed at bed time.

I am an avid reader and I read many books for work and pleasure. I reduce the expense of buying books by borrowing them from my local library. I developed my love of reading by going to the library as often as weekly in the summertime when I was a young child, and continued into my adult life primarily borrowing audio books to listen to on my long commute or when I was handling routine chores around the house. A library run can be a fun activity for the whole family. As much as I enjoy perusing the shelves to find a book, I no longer have the luxury of time. Instead, I download books to my mobile devices. Not only do I save time, the process could not be simpler and I will always have something to read or listen to at my fingertips.

Dine out less frequently and take advantage of the other services mentioned in this Chapter to eat healthy Eat breakfast at home and pack your lunch instead of eating out during the workday. You will help your waistline as well as your wallet. One of my friends started a new job and the norm for his colleagues was to eat lunch at a restaurant every day. My friend wanted to bond with his peers and felt compelled to join them in their daily ritual. This new practice caused my friend to gain weight quickly, which forced him to choose an alternative. He shared his problem with his co-workers and informed them he would bring his lunch every day except on Friday when he would join them for lunch. Of course, his colleagues were more than accommodating. The one day per week designated for my friend to participate, the group ensures healthy choices are available on the restaurant menu. These kind co-workers went even further and at times order carry out food so they can all sit and eat outside together when the weather is nice.

Ever since I committed to losing and sustaining a healthy weight, I bring my packed lunch almost everywhere. Even when I know lunch is available, I bring my own food. I will usually peruse the buffet line and maybe help myself to some salad to supplement my meal. I will admit that at first, I was worried that I would look like an outlier, but I learned quickly that no one cares that I am not eating the same food as the rest of the team. On more than one occasion, my teammates have commented on how much more appealing my lunch is than what is set before them! Packing my lunch helps me stay on track with healthy eating habits and has become second nature to me. I also feel good about the money I am saving that enables me to fund other activities in my life that are more important.

You will be more likely to get your work done during working hours if you avoid the traditional lunch outing. I am not suggesting you need to eat at your desk every day, although all the crumbs in my laptop and my very sticky keyboard are evidence that I am certainly guilty as charged on this count. I allot one half hour rather than a full hour for lunch every day. I get away from my desk to grab my lunch, have a quick conversation with one of my colleagues and then head back to my desk to eat and catch up on a few emails.

Packing your lunch (and breakfast or snacks) will save you a lot of money and will fund the outsourcing of a major activity. With the price of lunch ranging from a low of $5 for fast food to $12 for a sit down meal (yes these are Midwest prices), over the period of one year you can save from $1200 to almost $3000 per year! Even when you factor in the cost of purchasing your food at the grocery store the savings are substantial. You can easily fund a cleaning or lawn maintenance service.

A few other ideas for finding dollars to fund your outsourcing include:

Take the time to save money when shopping. You can quickly download e-coupons for grocery stores or sales at many retailers. As for clothes shopping, I buy fewer, better made clothes on sale and I mix and match them. My wardrobe consists primarily of black, navy and white. I watch for sales of clothes from brands or designers I know will fit me or reasonably priced items that that will last a long time. I stay away from the latest trends to ensure my choices will stand the test of time.

My accessories are limited as well. I have been wearing the same few pairs of earrings for the last ten to fifteen years. On a daily basis, I still use the wallet I purchased in 2002. I have a few purses, tote bags and backpacks I rotate through every few months. While no one has ever told me, "Wow! Aren't you wearing that latest designer blouse?" I receive compliments on my appearance and that is good enough for me. Cut back on your shopping habits as a means to fund your outsourcing. The bottom line is "buy less, buy to last, then reinvest in you!"

Use Woolite® or a home dry cleaning kit and save on the cost of the dry cleaner. This statement may appear to be in conflict with my earlier outsourcing comments; however, home dry cleaning is easy and saves a lot of time and money. You simply use the dry cleaning cloth to clean up any small stains then throw the garment into the dryer with the cloth for a few minutes. With most workplaces allowing more casual dress I find I have less need to take an article of clothing to a professional dry cleaning service. I also use a steamer to remove the wrinkles from my suits keeping them looking neat and clean. One caveat. Cotton shirts for my husband continue to go to the dry cleaner for laundering and pressing. I do not have the time nor the patience to tackle this task.

If you color your hair, you know how expensive and time consuming this practice can be. After two hours in the salon, you leave feeling like a million bucks . . . because it costs almost that much for a cut and color! Many good timesaving hair color products are available for use in the home. When you color your hair at home, you are free to tackle important tasks around the house. I recently pulled the plug on going to the salon simply because I could not consistently coordinate my travel schedule with that of my stylist. With her help, I chose an online service that delivers my color every few weeks. The total prep and processing time is the same as what I experienced at the salon. However, I am now able to roam around my home and tackles chores that need to be done while I am processing. In addition, I now color my hair on my schedule and do not have to rearrange other important matters to fit into the salon's schedule. I still visit my stylist every eight weeks for a haircut and she approves of the quality and look of the hair color.

If you are still unconvinced that you can afford to outsource, then swap services with your friends, family and neighbors. Agree to watch your friend's child on Saturday evening in exchange for her watching yours one night a week so you can finish college or graduate school. Ask your mother to make extra meals for the week and in turn take her along with you when you go grocery shopping so she can purchase her groceries at the same time.

Early on in my career, I did not have disposable income, which made financing an outsourced activity a challenge. To decrease my commuting expenses and free up funds, I participated in a car pool and parked in the lowest cost parking lot I could find. I had to take a short bus ride across the river and back into town then walk several blocks farther to get to my job, but the savings were worth it to ensure

I was not overextended and could pay for some of my outsourcing needs. I also swapped services with some of my friends. One year, I agreed to watch my friend's son several times so she could get her holiday shopping and baking done. In exchange, she made me a beautiful embroidered pillow to give as a gift to one of my relatives. Get creative and you will see that you can fund some of your outsourcing requests, even if it does not involve a monetary exchange.

Prioritizing your outsourcing list

How do you decide which activities to outsource? If you want to truly de-clutter and simplify your life, a deep review is required. Document your daily activities for two to four weeks, including all the purchases you make, bills you pay and tasks you perform. Include activities that seem to pop up out of nowhere, like unexpected trips to the grocery store, an extra takeout meal or entertainment activity, fund raising requests or other things out of synch with your usual routine. Capturing this information allows you to take a look at each task and activity that slips into your life planned or unplanned so you can determine which activities you should stop doing completely, those you should continue to perform yourself, and those you should outsource. This review will also give you an opportunity to understand how you are spending your hard-earned dollars and where you will be able to find the extra cash to fund your outsourcing.

OUTSOURCING

My husband and I were at dinner with friends recently (and yes, we genuinely enjoy their company) and they were asking my husband what he did all day since he retired. My husband and I gave examples of how he has been saving us money and he made the following comment, which I think is relevant to dual working couples. "When Beth and I were both working, we were focused on convenience. We took every opportunity to remove laborious or mundane activities from our plates. Now that I am retired, I have the time to focus on activities I believe will bring us real savings. We still outsource many activities that neither of us enjoy or, retired or not, are not worth my time." Well said.

"Don't be busy, be productive"

~Unknown

Chapter 6

Automate

The next best thing to outsourcing is automating. At the workplace, we search for ways to automate repeatable tasks to save time and focus our human capital on more important activities. You can automate in your personal life as well.

Bill paying. Begin with paying your bills. Put everything you can on auto-deduction from your checking account. I realize many people may struggle from paycheck to paycheck. I have been in this position myself when I was younger, but I would urge to you look at your expenses and see what you can cut out so you can be assured you will have sufficient funds in your account to pay your bills automatically. Setting up automatic bill paying is easy (a one-time form and a voided check) and will help you relieve stress.

Prior to her death, I helped my mother pay her bills. She was hesitant to move to automatic deduction because she said paying her bills in person gave her some interaction with the outside world. While I understood and appreciated her perspective, she was unable to write checks and this process quickly became a burden on me to handle. One Sunday afternoon I was rushing around my home trying to tie up some loose ends before catching a flight for work. I looked at the pile of my mother's bills sitting on my desk and I started to cry. I was overwhelmed with sorting through and paying all those bills by the traditional check writing method. Not only was this approach too time consuming, I was concerned I would not always be able to pay the bills on time as my work travel often kept me away from home two weeks at a time. I was worried that a late payment would place my mother and sister at risk. At that moment, I made an executive decision and enrolled in every automatic payment program available. Taking this action was the right thing to do for me and for her and it saved me from a lot of future stress and anxiety. To meet my mother's desire for socialization, I made sure on my visits to her home I would take my mother shopping or run small errands with her to get her out of the house.

If you have good financial discipline, link all your bills on your credit card and pay off the balance *every* month. This tactic allows you to keep your money in your interest-bearing accounts as long as possible and you can earn frequent flier miles toward free travel or other rewards. I have been able to cover the airfare and hotels for many trips by using this method. I also receive my bill notices via email so I can be sure the correct amount is charged. Because I travel extensively, I may not have access to traditional mail for weeks at a time. Online bill paying allows me to stay on top of my bills even when I am not at home.

If you do better making payments in smaller amounts, then consider simplifying the bill paying process and writing out your checks for bills on the first and the fifteenth of the month or every other week, if you receive a paycheck twice per month. You can make progress in paying your bills in an amount that is more amenable to your budget.

Lump sum payments. Paying for repeatable services in one lump sum can save both time and money. Most real estate, local income taxes, auto and home insurance and subscription services are typically bills you receive periodically that accept quarterly or annual payments. These lump sum payments usually come with a discount and that is money in your pocket (which helps pay for your cleaning service)! My sister, Teresa, likes receiving and reading the newspaper. I pay for an annual subscription, receive a discount, and do not have to worry about making a payment until the following year.

Routine online purchases. Most consumers are comfortable buying services online. Take advantage of this convenience and shift the products you buy repeatedly – household cleaning supplies, paper products and food staples. Buy nonperishable groceries such as condiments (ketchup, mustard, and mayonnaise) and cooking (spices) and baking (flour, sugar, salt) online. With delivery services such as Amazon Prime, the annual shipping fee is likely less than the gas and wear and tear on your car and online ordering is a better use of your time than traveling back and forth to the grocery store. Amazon's easy button automatically reorders for you when you are running low on certain products. Hit the "easy" button and your order is processed then delivered to your home, sometimes on the same day. In addition, most grocery stores now allow you to order online and pick up curbside, which helps you replenish your food supply regularly with minimal effort. Amazon also delivers fresh food to your home in many cities. In the summer, buy into a co-op that will deliver fresh fruits and vegetables to your door every week. You will get wholesome fresh foods without lifting a finger.

Booking multiple visits in advance. Along the line of automation is the idea of pre-scheduling recurring services so you establish a rhythm. As a female, I am sure you can appreciate how challenging it is to schedule a hair or nail appointment. The good stylists are booked for months in advance and it is almost impossible to get a cut and color on a moment's notice. Preplanning is the only way to get the services I want from my preferred stylist. Therefore, I schedule my hair appointments for a full year in advance and enter the information on my calendar, which allows me, for the most part, to ensure I don't have a conflict between my work does and my hair appointment. I schedule my nail appointments four to six visits in advance as that is typically as far out as my nail stylist takes appointments. Truthfully, if I were not working, I would stop getting my nails done all together as a means to save time and money. As I noted earlier, I have shifted to a home delivery service for quality hair color. For now, I need my nails done to maintain a professional appearance, so this service stays on my list on as an outsourced and automated activity. As I mentioned earlier, some women schedule their mammograms and routine gynecological exams on their birthdays every year so they never get off schedule. Think of automation as building a repeatable good habit to keep you on track for a simpler, less stressful life.

You can tap into your outsourcing partners to automate their schedule of activities. Our lawn service comes every Thursday like clockwork so we avoid having other contractors work on the same day. You can tell the window cleaners (at least for the outside job) to come every six months and the same applies to pest control, gutter cleaning, snow removal, etc. I ask all my home maintenance partners to simply put me on their schedule and send me the bill. You will be surprised how willing they are to accommodate you as a loyal customer.

Each of us has important personal events we must remember, birthdays, anniversaries, holidays and so on. The good news is these events come at the same time every year, and by automating, you can eliminate some of the last minute stress. For your mother's birthday, you can set a reminder to order flowers from the same company each year. The same applies to Professional Assistants or Bosses Day. Some service companies will store your important dates and set up automatic reminders. In addition, they store your past purchases so you know not to send the exact same gift year after year. Each year I receive an email notification from Lynch Creek Farms displaying their beautiful wreath selections. They make it easy for me to scroll through, choose a wreath and have it arrive at my door days later. I enjoy the opportunity to choose a different wreath each year, and appreciate how easy they make it for me to click and order which is why I buy from them almost every year.

Prescriptions present another opportunity for automation. Most health plans offer a mail order services with free delivery. In addition, some medications may be free of have a reduced copay when using mail order. Set the order up once per year and it arrives at your door every 90 days. Mail order relieves stress and can help lower your out-of-pocket healthcare costs.

"Though she bee but little, she bee fierce!"

~Unknown

Chapter 7

Just Say No

When my son was young, the Parent Teachers Association at his elementary school had many bake sales. Obviously, this was before gluten free, sugar free and healthier snacks became the norm. One day one of the mothers approached me about the bake sale, "Would you be willing to bake one or two dozen cupcakes?" she asked. I responded I might be able to swing by the grocery store and pick some up. From the shocked look on her face, you would have thought I was going to steal the cupcakes from the store. This mother very condescendingly informed me they only wanted home baked goods and if I was too busy to help my child's school out then that was fine. I felt guilty for a fleeting moment and then shrugged my shoulders and replied, "You're right, I am too busy." Then I turned and walked away.

This interaction was unusual for me. As an Obliger, I find it hard to say no to others. In my mind, I automatically elevate the requesting party to the Queen Bee, which means I feel an inherent obligation to meet the request. I often feel backed into a corner acquiesce to a request. I typically would make that meaningless commitment my priority, which usually resulted in not doing something more meaningful. Eventually, I did learn over the years how to prepare myself for these situations. When asked on subsequent occasions to bake, I just put it out there. "Sorry, I don't have time to bake, but I will be happy to contribute $10 to the bake sale. Does that work?" It only takes a minute for the other person to realize the whole purpose of the bake sale is to make money and that $10 is a good deal. I never receive a negative response to providing a check over volunteering my time.

As parents, we often donate our time to support our child's activities that may include coaching, chauffeuring kids to and from events, fundraising, and event set up and tear down and more. Recently I learned about a parental commitment, which sounded extraordinary to me, and frankly something to which I could never commit.

One night per week during high school football season, the parents must feed the team, the cheer squad *and* the coaching staff. The woman explaining this concept to me shared that she fed 140 individuals each week over the course of fourteen weeks. When I remarked that she must be a millionaire to afford all the food for so many growing teens, she further explained that the parent's role is to convince local restaurants to donate the meals. Apparently, this practice is prevalent, as another woman joined in the conversation and reinforced this practice. All I could think of was the time commitment required by these parents over the course of a single season. My hat is off to them for their dedication.

When your child commits to an activity, *you* commit to an activity. However, you can and should put parameters around your involvement in these activities. When our son was young, he played soccer, and at one point was interested in the traveling team. My husband said no to his request, and as we discussed it, I realized my husband was right in voicing his objections. As a member of the traveling squad, we would have been required to travel up to three hours each way, and this travel would have consumed most of our weekend. While initially disappointed, our son continued with the local team and had just as much fun.

When our son was in high school, he joined the crew team, which also traveled far distances. We supported him in this activity, which included bus transportation and overnight accommodations, all supervised by volunteer parents and paid for by us. Parents could volunteer to chaperone, which we never did, and I do not believe that made us bad parents. We did however, choose to drive several hours on more than one occasion to support and cheer him on. Our son enjoyed these trips and preferred taking the bus, which provided him some independence, time with friends and gave Mom and Dad a break too.

When choosing activities with your children, agree with them *before* you commit as to what you will and will not do. If you have an expectation that your children will share in some of the financial costs, let them know this expectation as part of the decision-making process so they understand whether they'll need to get a part-time job or use their birthday funds. Part of saying no is setting expectations up front.

Sometimes we insert ourselves into our children's activities. For example, we want our kids to succeed in school so we may participate in their projects more deeply than maybe we should. If your child is working on a craft project for school, let her determine how she wants her art to look. It may not be how you do it, but it is her project after all. There are times when your child really needs your help, but you might want to step back and see if he really needs assistance or if you are simply hovering, as many parents are often prone to do.

Another time trap seems to be the extension of work related team activities that encroach on your personal life. Team building is an important activity and you should participate as a colleague. You may find the need to draw the line and participate in activities that take place only during work hours. My work colleagues engage in many volunteer activities, and sometimes they take place in the evenings and on weekends. While I enjoy this time with my peers, I have learned that I need to limit my participation otherwise I over-commit. It takes its toll on me as I may fall behind in my work or not spend enough time with my family.

I have also experienced a unique situation over the years, which I would like to share. Because I commute to another city for my job, my husband and I are not in the same city during the week so we consider our weekends to be sacred time for the two of us. In my role, I often receive invitations to or am required to host events that take place over the weekend, usually involving the attendance of spouses. When my husband was also a senior executive, he made a decision that I fully supported. He chose not to take personal time off work to attend these events with me as his view was, "Why should I take time off work to watch you work?" I agreed, and unless my husband and I jointly decided to host an event at our home, I rarely attended his events. At times, I could tell my peers or guests would raise an eyebrow when once again, I arrived at a work-related event unescorted, but I did not let it phase me. I noticed that single women on the team had no requirement to appear with some arm candy, so I was not going to force my husband to take time off work to attend an event in which he was not interested. Saying no to these situations can be tough and often a bit political, but I held my ground and have no regrets. Based on where I stand with my career today, I am certain my decisions did not negatively affect my career over the long term.

Since I am a hopeless romantic, I almost hesitate teeing up the next two "just say no" activities, but here goes – weddings and showers. Over the years, I have been in several weddings and have hosted my fair share of bridal and baby showers. I urge you to think long about either of these activities. Being a bridesmaid is often a nightmare. The bride often embodies all the negative attributes of a Queen Bee, or in today's terms, a Bridezilla. The entire process is costly, time consuming and aggravating. You spend money on an ugly dress with dyed matching shoes that you will never wear again. You are asked to get your hair done in a special manner and have your nails polished. You have to wear something nice for the rehearsal dinner. Sometimes you have to travel far to get to the event incurring additional costs for airfare or gasoline and hotel rooms, not to mention the time away from work or your own family. Moreover, the time commitment required to working up to the big day can be onerous. You have to host the bridal shower, which costs you even more time and money. You spend countless hours with the bride looking at pictures of everything imaginable under the sun. I realize I must sound like a killjoy, but I have come to realize I have to be practical. One of my friends informed me that her child received invitations to quite a few weddings this year and her child is in several of these weddings. That is a lot of time, effort and money for a young person living on their own and trying to manage within a budget.

If your sister, brother, or best friend is getting married, then jump in with both feet and be as generous and supportive as you can. However, if it is your second cousin twice removed or someone you are no longer close to, I suggest you think long and hard and then decline the opportunity. In my opinion, I am not wasting my time and money on anyone who I do not consider my dearest of friends or family member.

My husband has a great approach to weddings. We attend the ceremony and we skip the reception. Yes, you read that correctly. We attend the wedding ceremony, and we receive appreciation from the bride, and groom because, other than their closest friends and family members, most guests usually skip the ceremony and head straight to the reception. The happy couple receives our best wishes in person at the church or temple, which is more meaningful. After the ceremony my husband and I either go out to a really nice dinner or we order take out and switch into comfortable clothes when we get home and watch a movie or do something else together. My husband started this practice after he grew tired of waiting hours to eat a cold, bland dinner at the reception and the portions were so small we often picked up fast food to fill our stomachs on the way home. He decided it was better to attend the ceremony and skip the dinner. I think this is a great approach and one that we follow with rare exception. Since we are dressed nicely for the ceremony, we often go to dinner and enjoy some alone time.

My attitude is the same for baby showers. They take a lot of time and coordination if you are hosting, and they usually take time away from your family even if you are only an attendee. I recall one conversation with several colleagues where they were saying how many wedding, bridal and baby showers they had attended. I shared the number of gifts I purchased and someone asked, "Oh, so you attended six events this year?"

"No," I replied, "I didn't attend *any* of these events. I simply purchased a gift on the registry and sent my blessings." My colleagues were shocked that I did not care to get a payback on my gift purchase by attending the event, eating, and drinking my heart out. I have no expectations that someone should be obligated to feed me because I chose to send a gift. I also don't feel obligated to send a gift because I simply received an invitation to a wedding or shower. I use my own values and judgment to determine when to say "Yes," or just say "no." I don't overcomplicate the decision.

In my quest to maintain my weight, the biggest challenge at weddings or showers I face is people, including friends or family members, pushing food at me all the time. They will say, "Just one little bite won't hurt," or, "Just this one time you don't have follow the plan." Most people mean well, at least I think they do, but they overstep their bounds. I don't feel an obligation to my friend, relative or host to eat everything on the buffet. In fact, I often take my own food with me to events. The inability to say "no" can have an impact on your ability to maintain a healthy lifestyle.

The key to saying "no" is preparation. You have to pre-formulate and practice phrases in your head that you can readily access in certain situations. For example, I often get women and men who reach out to me and ask me to be their mentor or their sponsor. Over the years, I have developed set responses. For example, I tell them, "I'm sorry I cannot be your sponsor. I only sponsor individuals I have worked with very closely over the years because I have to be confident in the quality of their work product, skills and commitment." With this concise but accurate explanation, the requestor understands why he or she would not be a good sponsorship candidate for me. As for the mentorship, I tell them I do not have the time to serve as a mentor but I am happy to spend twenty minutes with them to have a brief conversation about their career aspirations or to help them solve a problem. Sometimes my direct approach surprises people, but that is neither my problem, nor my fault. If I said yes to every request of my time, I would be deprioritizing matters that are more pressing.

In my line of work, I receive many dinner (and breakfast and lunch) invitations. In order to keep my weight and my sanity, I have learned several techniques. If you have someone who helps you manage your work schedule, let him or her know it is *never* okay to accept an invitation for any food based event (meals, after work drinks, coffee) without your permission. The reason I am so strict about food-based events is not only due to closely monitoring my weight, but also, these events represent a real time commitment. You may have to wait a few minutes until a table is ready, then peruse the menu, order, wait to receive your meal, eat it, wait for the bill, wait for the bill to be processed and then finally you are free to leave. The entire process is exhausting and if you have limited time or do not really connect with the person you are with, you have not spent your time well.

When you receive an invitation, determine if this is really someone you have to go to dinner with, whether you can delegate or just pass. For example, if a client is coming into town, I am more willing to have dinner if I know I am not spending time with them in a meeting the next day. If a business partner wants to have dinner, I apply the same criteria. I refuse to have meals with external sales representatives as an example. In fact, I refuse meetings with these individuals in general because these meetings are not a good use of my time. Instead, I ask them to send me information, which I do review, and I agree to get back with them if I or someone else within the organization is interested in learning more.

I often have work colleagues who want to grab a quick bite to eat. Unless I feel like I need to build the relationship or it is someone whose company I really enjoy (and who will not spend most of the dinner talking about work), I decline the invitation. If I you are not discerning in your acceptance, you may find your calendar overscheduled with meaningless and time wasting events. Remember, saying "no" is harder than saying yes but it is crucial to helping you achieve balance in your life.

I also look at the number of events I have committed to in any given week and try to limit to no more than two lunches or dinners. When I travel into the field, I like to spend time over a meal with my team, but I have learned over the years when I arrive at 6:30 pm and have a dinner scheduled for 7:30 pm I am too tired to participate at the top of my game. I routinely say no to the dinner invitation and instead I get a good night's sleep and meet with my team over breakfast. I am a morning person so I know I show up better for these types of events, incur less expense, and am more apt to watch my caloric intake.

Another "just say no" trick is to attend cocktails only and exit as others move to the table for dinner. This approach permits me to interact with people for a designated time without committing my entire evening. Recently I felt obligated to attend a celebratory dinner hosted by an external business partner. Cocktails lasted an hour and a half, and an hour into the dinner I was getting cranky. When I saw the staff bringing out the desserts I jumped up, informed my colleagues I had a very early meeting and joked that since I am a lifetime Weight Watchers member I was running from dessert. My statement received a good chuckle and I am sure no one took offense at my slightly early retreat.

Always be on the lookout for an early escape from an event. Most of the entertaining I do is part of my job, and while I very much enjoy the company of others, I know that to do my job properly I need to depart at a reasonable time to ensure I get my rest. I am so good at getting out of events quietly and without offending others that I find my colleagues asking me to let them know when I am leaving so they can join me in my escape. I have learned over the years that dinners or other evening events are not just taxing on me they also create a burden for many of the other attendees, who have commitments outside of work. I find that the team really just wants to spend time with me and that interaction can happen during business hours and be very effective.

I have mentioned multi-tasking several times as a means quickly to check items off my list. I stand by the concept of multitasking for many reasons; however, there is a time and a place where multitasking may not be the best choice and falls into the "just say no" category. When you really need to focus, whether it is during a conversation with someone, or you need to concentrate on completing a specific project, do not attempt to multitask. Rid yourself of all potential distractions. Turn off your email notifications or your phone. Close your door and hold your calls. Focusing on the task you have prioritized allows you to complete it faster with better results.

Just saying "no" requires you to plan ahead to respond appropriately to requests for your time, exit events or avoid unwanted food or alcohol. Having a few tried and true statements in your back pocket allows you to bow out gracefully and keeps good relations intact. Remember, when you say "no" to one thing, you free up time to say "yes" to other more meaningful activities.

"You can do anything but not everything."

~Unknown

Chapter 8

Overscheduling

Nothing brings out the true character of a Busy Bee more than her schedule. We brag how busy we are, how many tasks we have yet to accomplish and how many activities we juggle simultaneously. Silly, silly, Busy Bee! You may think busy-ness translates to self-importance, but this is no longer the case. When I hear someone talk about how busy their personal life is I think to myself, "This person cannot get her act together." Hearing busy talk does not make me want to be your friend because you would never have the time commitment to be a true friend. I don't want to be your work colleague either because I need to count on colleagues who are efficient and organized and not individuals who will risk throwing an entire project off kilter because she doesn't know how to prioritize and focus. When you brag about your busy schedule, and most of us are guilty of this, you publicly brand yourself as a Busy Bee and it can hinder your professional career and your personal relationships.

You can regain control of your life! Stop overscheduling yourself and your kids. As parents, we want to give our kids the advantages we never had, so we often encourage them to try many extracurricular activities. Children have numerous options today – sports, music lessons, dance, 4H, the science club, and many, many more. Don't be a tiger mom! Limit activities to two or three per child. Remember, you have to shuttle little Johnny to and from these activities, so Johnny's activity now becomes your activity.

Begin to assess your schedule by writing down all (yes, ALL) the activities in which your child participates outside of her normal school day. Staying after school once per week to work on the school newspaper counts as one activity. Church is an activity. If your son watches the neighbor's children every Saturday night, it counts as an activity. Walking the neighbor's dog after school, playing sports, and yes, even going to Grandma's house every Sunday for dinner counts as an activity.

All these activities require time commitment including traveling to and from the activity as well as the activity itself. If the activity has a substantial time commitment like a traveling soccer team, you might want to count that activity as two. If you are convinced your daughter is the next David Beckham then go for it! Otherwise, stick with the non-traveling team. Conversely, you might want to count a limited time activity (less than a half-hour each week including travel time) as half of an activity.

Make decisions as a family as to which activities are viable options for your kids. Make sure they choose the activities about which they are passionate or select activities that will help advance them in life. When choosing activities with your kids (and you should clearly weigh in given your time commitment) think about and discuss with your child the benefits of that activity. If your child is shy (or perhaps an only child) and you want to put him in an environment where he can consistently engage with others, then a team sport might be a good option. If your child lacks confidence about her abilities then perhaps a sport like cross country or bowling, where the competition is her own prior performance, might be best. Be sure to include activities that benefit the entire family. For example, if both your kids like to swim and their practices are at the same time, this makes life easier for everyone. You will need to help your child choose among the many options available to them, so take the process of selecting your child's activities seriously because their commitment is your commitment.

Your schedule

I enjoy watching romantic comedies as they provide me with a small respite from all the busy-ness that surrounds me. In the movie *27 Dresses*, one scene stands out in my mind and represents how we overschedule ourselves. After escorting actor Katherine Heigel's character home in a taxi, Tom Marsden finds Katherine's Filofax on the taxi seat. When he peeks inside he cannot believe how packed her schedule is and that she actually participated in two weddings in one day! I can relate, not to attending two weddings in a single day, but I was guilty of jamming my weekdays and weekends so full, I didn't have any down time.

At one point, I was waking up at 5:00 am and arriving in the office between 6:30 am and 7:00 am. I convinced myself I wanted to arrive early to avoid traffic and this statement was partially true. My early morning schedule also had me avoiding exercise. At this time in my life, I was telling myself I was a morning person and morning was the only time I could exercise. Of course, I didn't have enough time to go to the gym and exercise, then get ready and drive into the office before rush hour. Since I did not exercise much and had poor eating habits, I gained weight.

To exacerbate further the problem, I routinely scheduled meetings as early as 7:00 am. I would work through lunch and typically end my last meeting around 6:00 pm, which resulted in eleven hours of work without a break. I'd leave the office at 6:30 pm and by that time I was too exhausted to cook, so I'd order dinner from the drive-thru, take-out or if I was being exceptionally lazy I would have food delivered. I felt totally justified ordering out because my schedule was so crazy (of course by my own volition). Finally, I would work until at least 11:00 pm then get up and do it all over again the next day. I was on the proverbial treadmill, when I needed to be on a real treadmill.

I used overscheduling as an excuse or crutch to justify not putting myself first. As a result I lacked sleep and was a cranky boss (I am sure many of my colleagues will attest to my cranky demeanor), and was damaging my health in the process. I did this to myself for over twenty years. It is a wonder I didn't die of a heart attack! I have changed my schedule significantly in the last ten years. I rarely take a meeting before 8:30 am, and I now end meetings no later than 5:30 pm. I block off Friday afternoons for several hours so I can clean up loose ends. Using this time wisely allows me to head into the weekend feeling good about my accomplishments and not worrying about unfinished work. These were conscious decisions I had to make to block this time on my schedule. You may think it is easy for me to control my calendar because I am an executive, but it can really be a challenge. While my calendar still fills with meetings, I am now successful at maintaining the block of hours during which I will take a meeting because I protect my time, as does my assistant.

Several years ago, I decided to take a stand and protect my weekends. The inciting incident happened on an Easter Sunday. I was online catching up on emails. (You are reading this correctly, I was *working* on Easter). I was monitoring an exchange of emails initiated by my manager at the time. He admonished us for failing to comment on a Power Point document we had received around 10 pm on Good Friday. We had an important presentation the Monday after Easter, and my manager wanted to ensure the presentation would go smoothly. I remember being irritated at the expectation we should be working on a holiday.

I continued to stew over my manager's unrealistic expectations during the next few weeks. One day I had an epiphany. I was attending a workshop where

I heard the terms "Digital Sabbath" and "Digital Detox" and my ears perked up. These concepts involve individuals stepping away from their electronic devices for a period, perhaps during dinner, one evening a week or over the weekend. I clearly remember how my peers let the idea pass but I clung to the notion of real downtime on the weekends. I turned this idea over repeatedly in my head and was excited to share this concept with my team.

As I was thinking about the idea of Digital Detox, I came to a stark realization. If my manager was the biggest offender in the company by virtue of sending a large number of emails on weekends, I was certainly the second worst offender. Truthfully, I might have been the worst offender. It was perfectly normal for me to generate 150 – 200 emails each weekend, which caused my team to be online ensuring they responded at the latest, Monday morning. I realized I would have to change my personal habits significantly if I were to succeed in instituting a Digital Detox. I would also have to make sure my team was willing to participate.

At my next staff meeting, I raised the idea of Digital Detox. I expected my team to be thrilled and want to implement this program immediately. I was wrong. The team was very hesitant about implementing Digital Detox. I was perplexed. I could not imagine why anyone would pass on an opportunity for some weekend down time.

Why were they concerned? Many companies operate in a 24/7 culture and our organization is no exception. The expectation is that we respond to emails in the evenings, on weekends, during vacations and holidays. We are in an "always on" environment. My team feared we would appear to be less engaged or less valuable if we did not abide by this unwritten norm. More importantly, the team was fearful they would bear the anger of my manager if they did not respond promptly to every email he sent, whether or not it was after normal work hours. Finally, we had some work areas, such as our call center that did have extended business hours so people needed to stay connected.

We found solutions to each of these concerns. To avoid the appearance of being slackers we decided to embark on Digital Detox but not share our decision with the rest of the company. I have learned over the years that, at times it's best to take action now and ask for forgiveness later. I then had a conversation with my manager, told him about our little experiment and my team's concerns that he would be angry and think poorly of them for not responding immediately to one of his requests. To my great surprise he said, "I don't expect people to respond to me on the weekends." I was smart enough not to reference the Easter Sunday event during our conversation. To address the final issue of our extended operational needs, we proposed using text messaging for communicating an emergency. Since most people have their phones with them, this approach ensured they would respond quickly, but at the same time, ensured the individual would not have to check emails throughout the weekend.

Our team decided to move forward with our experiment in May 2014. We announced the implementation of our new Digital Detox program to all our associates just before Memorial Day and agreed to extend it through Labor Day. The guidelines were simple. Refrain from sending emails between the hours of 6:00 pm Friday through 6:00 am Monday based on the associate's local time zone. Exceptions for critical activity or busy times such as during budget prep season were acceptable, but these exceptions required advanced vetting.

The positive response to this change by our associates was unbelievable. I received numerous thank you notes and heard stories about how the receipt of an email on the weekend in the past might have ruined someone's entire weekend if they thought the sender was upset with them. Others told me how they had felt tethered to their phones and really did not feel present in their family activities. One associate shared, "You gave me my life back. Thank you."

While it took some time for some of my leaders to adapt to this change I held firm, calling them out when they broke the rules by sending an email for a routine matter on the weekend. I even went so far as to tell spouses and partners at a sales event about the Digital Detox program. I could tell by the looks on their faces that it was clear some of our employees were not adhering to the practice. At the end of the summer trial period, we asked associates if they wanted to make the Digital Detox a permanent part of the culture in our segment and received a resounding positive response. This program continues today and I credit it with helping our segment achieve the highest employee engagement scores in the company.

I also began sharing our practice with other areas and repeatedly receiving applause for caring about the well-being of our associates. While the rest of our company has not officially adopted Digital Detox, the program clearly has had an impact not only in reducing the number of emails sent on weekends, but also in helping our employees achieve a certain level of well-being. My current manager, the CFO is well aware that my team has implemented this program and if he has an urgent matter to discuss with me he calls or texts me because he knows I am not constantly checking my emails on the weekend.

As for the concern that a team employing a Digital Detox strategy consists of a bunch of slackers, nothing could be further from the truth. Our performance results speak for themselves. We have consistently and at times significantly, outperformed our goals since implementing Digital Detox. Personally, I have learned to be much more efficient during the week knowing I am not going to be responding to emails on the weekend. For you skeptics, no I do not work in stealth mode all weekend. On those rare occasions when I do have to catch up, at the most I may have twenty emails that I prepare and save for release on Monday morning. By not responding to emails on the weekends, I have more free time to catch up on reading, exercise and generally invest in myself and I believe I am a better performer at work because now I have time to recharge my batteries.

What about you? Have you packed your work and personal schedules so tightly that, at times, you feel you can't even breathe? Do you have a problem saying "no" to invitations in and outside of work? Are your kid's activities consuming most of your time outside the office? Time to grow a backbone! Focus on activities that help keep your family together, benefit your career or fulfill your passion. For me these activities include hockey games with my husband, dinner with people I really care about or want to get to know better, healthy cooking and baking, exercising, reading and writing!

I was not always clear on which activities would benefit me personally and professionally. I was far from discerning in choosing what to put on my schedule. I believe the reason my schedule was so crammed and my work spilled over into the weekends was because I found it particularly challenging to say "no" to anyone. At one point, an internal audit revealed I was on more work committees than any other leader in the entire organization. For a fleeting moment, I was proud and then I realized I was sitting among a group of peers and superiors who were not handling the same workload as me yet they too were vice presidents or had even higher positions within the company. My ego deflated quickly when I realized more is not better. Now I realize I simply wasn't smart enough to prioritize my time and activities. I have since learned my lesson.

In deciding which activities to prioritize, think carefully about trade-offs. What does participating in a book club offer you? If it is networking to further your career then it's a great place to focus, but would grabbing a quick cup of coffee provide you a better networking opportunity? Would participation in a cross functional team at work provide you with the best networking opportunity?

If the purpose of the book club is mostly for getting away with the girls for a few hours, great, we all need time with friends. What other opportunities do you have to connect with friends that might not require a significant time commitment (reading the book, buying the food and wine for the book club, traveling to and from the host's home, talking for two plus hours)? That is quite a commitment.

I had a dear friend in human resources and we worked closely together for years on our employee benefits offering. Given the large number of associates we employed, we both spent a great deal of time and effort on this initiative. When I lived in Boston and commuted to Louisville, I usually worked from home on Fridays. My friend and I would arrange a debrief call every Friday late in the afternoon to ensure we were on top of all activities and on the same page. We first took care of any outstanding business issues on this call and then used the remaining time, if any, to chat as friends do. Our alternative would have been to separate these two activities which means with our schedule, we likely would not have been able to catch up on the friends part of our relationship as often.

Weigh your options and stack rank your activities among the others that will provide you with similar outcomes (networking, joy, silence), and then choose. You can't do everything, or at least you can't do everything well. You may have heard the phrase "fewer, bigger, better." I find doing fewer, more meaningful things provides me with a greater sense of fulfillment than checking the box off a long list of less than meaningful activities.

"That which is not good for the beehive is not good for the bees."

Marcus Aurelius

Chapter 9
Location, Location, Location

We have all heard the saying that location is of critical importance when starting a retail business. A convenient location is important in organizing our lives because you save time when it is close by or delivered to your door. Make a list of important activities or services you rely on that are located more than ten minutes from home or work. This list might include items like doctors and dentist offices, healthcare facilities, dry cleaners, hair salons, coffee shops, grocery stores, retail stores, fast food restaurants and so on. Determine if suitable alternatives are available. Another way of looking at convenience is to have the goods or services come to you. Listed below are examples of services where convenient locations or home delivery can save you time and money.

Doctors, dentists and healthcare facilities – Look for medical complexes housing a variety of specialty practices in one campus. Typically, you can find a primary care physician, pediatrician, OB/GYN, mammography facilities, urgent care and other specialties such as allergists in a centralized area. The campus approach makes it easy for you to schedule routine, annual appointments on the same day. Alternatively, look for offices located within ten minutes of your home. My primary care physician, OB/GYN, dentist and allergist are located less than ten minutes from my home and are in walking distance of each other. For someone who travels extensively, I highly recommend a concierge medicine practice. These practices cost more, but your doctor will accommodate you at a moment's notice, and will do a great job of ensuring you can get in and out of the office quickly. If you are traveling, your doctor may accommodate you with a virtual visit. If your doctor does not offer virtual services, plenty of other organizations provide telemedicine visits for a reasonable fee. If your illness is routine, pop into a clinic located inside your local grocery store or pharmacy. Some doctors are willing to make in-home visits for services such as a sick child or to give the family flu shots. Your employer may also offer services such as onsite clinics, mammograms and flu shots and often, these services are free. Do not wait until you are sick to check out these services. Make sure you know what options are available to you and become familiar with them so you know where to go when the need arises. Pre-planning and convenience really pay off when it comes to healthcare.

Grocery stores – Grocery stores now include dry cleaners, pharmacies, banks and much more. I recently learned about a jewelry store located inside a grocery store. (No Cracker Jack jokes, please)! Consider consolidating as many of your errands into a single location as possible. If you don't like shopping for groceries use the store's home delivery as an alternative. Grocery delivery has dramatically improved over the years. You can order your food online, and have it delivered to your home or you can pick it up at the store at a time specified by you. Grocery stores have overcome consumer's concerns over receiving poor quality meats, produce or other food close to expiration by training their staff to choose the highest quality when filling orders. Grocery delivery costs very little and is worth the time saved.

Dry cleaning – Use the grocery store dry cleaner or better yet, find one that picks up and delivers to your home. Another cheaper solution is the home dry cleaning kit, which is much less expensive and does not take much time or effort. My dry cleaner also does alternations and shoe repairs and yes, the dry cleaner is located within five minutes of my house. It is open at 7:00 am so I can run this errand and get back to my desk in time for my first meeting.

Pharmacy – Shift all the drugs you take on a routine basis such as cholesterol or blood pressure lowering drugs to the mail order pharmacy through your health plan or another discount website. You can order and refill online (most have automatic refill capabilities), and in many cases you save money because your copay is reduced for the larger quantity. Some local pharmacies have also introduced home delivery, which is particularly convenient when you do not want to drag a sick child out of the house to get a prescription filled.

Hair & nail salons – Most of us have a favorite stylist for our hair and nails. I am always amazed at how difficult it is to get an appointment. In addition to scheduling my appointments well in advance as I mentioned in Chapter 6, I ensure that these services are located within ten minutes of my house. If you use these services infrequently and are willing to take a chance, schedule these appointments when you are traveling. I have had my hair both cut and colored and my nails polished in airport and hotel salons and have rarely been disappointed. A friend of mine schedules a blow out when she travels so her hair looks fabulous for the few days she is away and she a to haul avoids the need to haul hair products with her on the trip. As an alternative, you can color your own hair at home. It is cheaper, much less time consuming and you can multitask during the coloring process.

Coffee Shops – I am always surprised at the long lines at the local coffee shops in the morning. I understand some people really need their coffee, but I struggle to understand why someone would spend 10 – 15 minutes waiting in line to pay $3 - $5 for a cup of java. How much time and money are you wasting sitting in the drive thru line at the Starbucks, Peet's Coffee, Dunkin' Donuts or Tim Horton's? No doubt, some of you will explain you are productively using this time to respond to emails or some other form of multitasking. Are you using this waiting time as wisely as possible? You can make your coffee at home while you are getting ready in the morning, pour it into a nice thermos and off you go. Maybe you like having the look of a fresh brewed latte in a nicely decorated disposable cup. I understand Starbucks is a status symbol and feels like a reward for your hard work. While I do not drink coffee I do love hot chocolate, so on a cold morning, I make myself some hot chocolate, put it in a pretty cup, snap a lid on it and take it with me to the office or when running errands. I feel as if I have given myself a treat without the expense of Starbuck's and I save time as well. If you insist on spending $15 a week on coffee, then try to find a coffee haven that is both convenient and has fast service, which may be the one closer to the office. If you must have your Starbucks, use the app to preorder and save some time.

Fast food – We all know most fast food is not good for us but fast food is a practicality of life. Sometimes we just can't find the time to cook and fast food is a way to get food quickly into our hungry family's tummies. While we should probably be eating as little fast food as possible, it is smart to have your go to chain that serves somewhat healthy options. For the kids, you can get grilled chicken nuggets instead of breaded at some chains and you can substitute apple slices for fries. Wraps and salads are a reasonable alternative for the grown-ups. You can consider pairing fast food with some healthier options at home. For example, get a grilled chicken sandwich, skip the side of fries and steam some broccoli at home as the side. Use fast food when you need to, just be mindful of what you are ordering and don't over-do it.

Retailers -- I live near a fabulous shopping mall and recently I remarked to my husband I had only been to this mall once since the prior Christmas and the reason was to eat breakfast at a local restaurant. Although at times I do like to see and feel the merchandise, attempting to squeeze shopping time in during an evening or a weekend is just too hard. My time is precious so I rarely spend it shopping at the mall on weekends. I usually do my shopping when I am on vacation or have an out of town work event that lasts several days and includes some free time. Recently, I was speaking at an event. I was the last speaker of the day, which meant I had an hour and a half window between the end of my presentation and the required dinner later that evening. I spotted one of my favorite department stores a block away and used that open time slot to sneak in and look at the merchandise. Having that store close by afforded me the opportunity to use an open time slot to tackle a task quickly that would otherwise consume a great deal of my time. I chose to have my order shipped to my home free of charge so I would not have to find room in my suitcase. Depending on where you live, you might also be able to save on sales tax. Location is important in saving time, energy and money.

My approach to shopping can be summed up in two words – quick and discount! Like many of you, I prefer to buy on sale and limit my time and effort by shopping online. Shopping is no longer a recreational activity for me. I recall one morning while reading my personal email a sale alert popped up on my screen. I scanned the retailer's website and ordered a dress online at 5:30 am. Unfortunately, my credit card company declined the transaction thinking it was a fraudulent request! Now they know me a little better and understand my online shopping habits are suited to my timetable (and yes, I was able to purchase the dress)!

Books – I really enjoy the experience of looking for a book and holding it in my hands while I am reading. I was a late adopter to e-books because I shared all my non-fiction books with my sister and donated the business books to the library at work. My sister has since received a Kindle; our company no longer has a library, so the need for hardback and paperback books has significantly dwindled. The most important location for books is now my Kindle, Barnes and Noble or Amazon app. Because I can download a book wherever I am (even at 30,000 feet in the air), I am never without reading material. While I occasionally still enjoy going to a retailer to buy books, it consider this time spent a luxury and something that I do infrequently.

Movies – Going to the movies is a great family activity and so is watching one at home. Not only is the latter less expensive, it saves time and typically offers more comfortable seating and better snacks. Now that new movies are available on demand shortly after a new theater release, your family can watch the most recent flicks without the hassle of going to the theater. Make it a special treat for your family to go to the movies at home. Buy a bag of pre-popped popcorn and some other goodies to make the event feel special. You will spend quality time together and make wonderful memories in the process. Save the trip to the movie theater for those blockbusters that require the big screen to fully appreciate the special effects, and for the other movies, snuggle up on the couch and enjoy the show at home.

All of these suggestions are designed to bring activities as *close to you as possible*, to save you precious time as well as money. Location really matters in simplifying our lives. As many routine activities you can manage in close proximity to or directly in your home, the better. Remember, there is no place like home and at the same time, know that simplifying and streamlining these routine activities allows you more time and freedom to wander farther from home for bigger adventures.

"There is nothing perfect . . . only life."

Sue Monk Kidd

Chapter 10

I'm Perfect . . . You're Not

In addition to our desire to balance an overwhelming number of activities in our lives, we Busy Bees like to think of ourselves as perfectionists. We are proud when someone says we have high standards, but should we proudly fly this flag of perfection? Let's dig a little deeper.

I'm perfect . . . you're not. We send this message every time we intervene in someone else's work. Face it. Many of us intervene, or to be a bit harsher, interfere, all the time, even in the tiniest details. Are you unsure this personality trait applies to you? You might be a perfectionist if you:

. . . rearrange the grocery cart when shopping with your spouse or partner.

. . . reposition your knick-knacks after your cleaning professional completes his work.

. . . secretly refold the towels after your son or daughter has already folded the laundry.

. . . routinely revise your team's work products multiple times.

. . . claim none of your staff can get the assignment right without significant input from you.

. . . feel proud that your standards are *exceptionally* high.

Do any of these sound familiar to you? I have been, and much to my chagrin, still am a perfectionist. Being perfect takes away from our precious time and our peace of mind. Frankly, it hurts the people who are targets of our perfectionism. If I failed to make the bed each morning, I would feel bad. Now I only make the bed when company is coming in case my visitor decides to be nosy. I pick my battles. I determine what looms large and important in my mind as the "big stuff" and what I consider the "small stuff." To be on my game and focused I know I have to have some semblance of order in my life, and that starts at home. While I know nothing can be perfect, I cannot live in a state of chaos. At home, I consider organization to be the "big stuff" and following are a few examples.

I generally allow a few pairs of my shoes to accumulate on the floor in the mudroom and anything over that amount moves to the hall closet. You may think I am being silly with this example and that it is not an example of the "big stuff," but please read on. I enter and exit my home through the mudroom, and if I am tripping over shoes and other clutter at the beginning or end of my day, it creates a negative tone that stays with me. When I arrive home to clutter I get edgy and the streak of perfectionism in me comes to the forefront. I have arranged my mudroom so it is very easy and natural to put things away rather than allow clutter to build up. I have drawers in the mudroom dedicated to holding hats, gloves and scarves. I hang large winter coats immediately because a big closet is available. I have an unattractive but very practical mat on the floor to collect dirt from our shoes and boots.

Food is the next major category of perfection for me. I cannot stand the thought of decaying food in my refrigerator and I have witnessed several people dealing with food poisoning, so I want to avoid food-based illnesses at all costs. If the refrigerator starts to smell bad, I immediately investigate and start tossing items growing fuzz or oozing liquid. Tying into my spoiled food issues, I do not allow dishes to sit in the sink overnight. I may wait an hour or more to clean up after dinner, but I do clean the kitchen every night and the dishwasher is loaded. I regularly remove the trash as the possibility of seeing ants crawling around my kitchen searching for food makes me shudder.

The last two non-negotiable items are a clean house and clean laundry. A clean home allows me to think more clearly, probably because subconsciously I recognize it is one less task for me to put on my list. I learned at an early age to either properly fold or hang my clothes up immediately after laundering or I would have to spend a lot of time ironing which is not something I enjoy. This habit has stayed with me through the years. As a professional it is important to me to have clean and pressed clothes (or at least not wrinkled if they are permanent press), because I feel better and have more confidence in myself. Trust me, if you are wearing wrinkled or less than freshly laundered clothes at work, people will notice. When I was in college, I worked in a professional office and I noticed one of the executives had ring around the collar caused by her foundation makeup rubbing off on her very expensive silk blouse. I remember thinking how dirty this otherwise professional woman looked. I took this lesson to heart and always ensure my clothes are always neat and clean.

Below are some examples of the "small stuff' items that I no longer worry about.

- I have come to realize my husband's office is his domain and have agreed to touch nothing! For the life of me, I cannot figure it out but he has his system and it seems to work. I offered to clean his office, and as you can imagine he declined my offer. Now I ignore any small piles he has on his desk. As long as the bills are paid (and almost everything is automated) and he can find whatever he needs and he does, I don't let this less than perfect office bother me!

- Car keys, prescription bottles, phone cords can all hang out on the kitchen counter as long as they do not interfere with the food prep area.

- I no longer care when someone folds the bath towels in a manner different than I prefer. I also do not care if the towels do not hang perfectly on the towel rack. Wow! Is that progress or what?

- I allow clutter on the top of my home office desk but clean it off by the time I leave for work on either Sunday night or Monday morning. At work, I straighten my desk at work each evening before I leave the office.

- I no longer seek to reorganize the loaded dishwasher, nor do I pull out the plates and utensils placed in the dishwasher without rinsing.

- I have given up any attempt to have an organized refrigerator, freezer or pantry. As long as I can quickly locate what I need, I overlook the disorganization.

- I now understand that when my husband does the laundry he will never understand that a sports bra goes into the drawer with my other workout clothes and does not go into the bra drawer. I have learned to look in many drawers to find my stuff. Similarly, my color coded/short hang/long hang/work/ casual closet system seems to work only for me so I have resigned myself to live with an imperfect closet!

The "small stuff' seems silly now, but at one time it was a much bigger deal to me because I was dealing with the perfect storm which happens when overscheduled and overworked meet perfectionism. Thankfully, I made a choice to enjoy the time I have with my family and stop fretting over meaningless issues. To help me tamp down on some of my perfectionist tendencies I did determine organization was critical, but I simplified my perception and approach.

What helps me control chaos is to have plenty of "in your face" storage systems. By putting baskets on counters, designating drawers for specific items and installing closets and other organizing systems, I have been able to control the chaos. When we lived in Boston, we had only a few hooks in the mudroom, which limited the amount of space for hanging coats. In addition, at that time my husband wore a suit to work every day. He would take off his coat and suit jacket and hang them on the back of the stools at the kitchen island. I could not stand this mess so I had a large hall closet installed specifically designed to hold both his overcoat and suit coats and it worked beautifully. No more suit coats in the dining room, and no more nagging my husband who was exhausted from a long day at the office.

I put baskets in places where I see "things" sitting. I have a tray where I place my jewelry (watch, wedding ring, earrings and Fitbit) each night. I keep my jewelry very simple and wear the same things repeatedly. The tray allows me to keep some order on my dresser and allows easy access in the morning when I am ready to put the jewelry back on. In my home office, I have drawers with organized compartments so I can quickly find and then return an item to its proper place.

Putting items away after immediate use is important as a means to avoid chaos.

I commute to work in another city and have two residences, one of which is a small condominium. I have neither the space nor the desire to duplicate everything I have in my home, so I have had to look for less expensive but equally effective organizing solutions for this tiny unit. Since I do not have an office in my condo, I use my kitchen and/or coffee table to spread out my work. I have note pads and pens, scissors and tape – all the usual items found in a well-stocked office. I bought two pretty boxes at a local discount store and place all my office supplies and television remotes there each night. These boxes hide the junk, serve as a nice accessory, and give me a little bit of control in an otherwise chaotic world.

Perfection at work

When you correct or redo a task, someone else believes she has completed to both her and your satisfaction you are sending a clear message – your efforts were not good enough. Her attempt to complete the report, or draft the presentation does not meet your high expectations, so she feels like a failure or an idiot. If someone has truly done a poor job or then you should fix it. If a presentation has spelling or grammatical errors it then change it, but this example is very straightforward. Most of the time perfectionists are not working with black and white subject matters but are working in the gray zone.

The product presented may have in fact satisfied the requirement, but may not have met the perfectionist's high standards.

As a reforming perfectionist who is still learning to let go, I try to set guidelines around what I will and will not change at work. If the work product contains grammatical or spelling errors, change it. If I am producing a document for the Board of Directors, my manager or a client, then I allow myself license to fret over fonts, colors, layout and words. However, I have learned, albeit the hard way, to let go of many other opportunities to raise the bar. While I applauded myself for my high standards, my team thought I was a perfect jerk. Their view was "good enough" should have been acceptable to me. In many cases, they were right. I had to learn as long as we got to the desired endpoint, it should not matter if a team member or colleague took a different approach. Over time, I realized I could learn a lot from looking at these different approaches. My altered view did not mean I abdicated responsibility for reviewing and ensuring a good work product. I simply had to learn and accept when someone else's work was good enough.

Years ago, my husband and I were having breakfast at a local restaurant. I was reading the book <u>The No A**hole Rule</u> by Robert Sutton. Early in the book, Sutton presents a quiz to determine whether you are an – well, you know. I took the quiz in my head and I smiled as I lowered the book. My husband sat across the table engrossed in reading something on his iPad.

I excitedly said to him, "Honey, I just took the a**hole quiz in this book and guess what? I'm not an a**hole!" My husband looked up from his iPad, looked me directly in the eye, and said, "Keep reading." While I look back and laugh at this incident now, I remember being slightly shocked and hurt at the time. Surely I couldn't be that bad, but I knew deep down that I had more than my fair share of a**hole moments. My desire for perfection was driving a lot of this behavior. No one is as honest with you as the ones you love, and I thank God my husband was honest that day.

Perfection at home

Perfection permeates your work and home life. Despite your belief to the contrary, you *are* the same person at work and home. If you are striving for perfection at home, you are criticizing the ones you love. This criticism may be direct or it may be indirect. Either way it hurts. I get my perfectionism streak from my mother who likely got it from her grandfather who she said was a tough person. I do not believe she intended criticism; rather, I believe this was her way of helping me learn life's lessons and preparing me for the real world. One year my sister and I decided we would decorate the Christmas tree. My mother was working at the time and we thought we were being helpful by taking on this responsibility. When my mother saw the tree, she was not happy. She let us know our work was sloppy and she would have to take everything off and redecorate again. We were both hurt and questioned why we had even bothered decorating the tree. Looking back, I don't think my mother intended to hurt our feelings. She was probably exhausted from a long day at work and overreacted. I wonder how many times we have hurt someone we love because we redid the task they had just completed. Each time we rework a task completed by another, we send a hurtful message of "not good enough," and take on more work than we need.

Where does this desire for perfection come from? Many times, it comes from our childhoods. We may have watched our mothers go to extraordinary lengths to take care of our family. If your mother or grandmother's work was exclusively rooted in the home, you might have high standards. I remember my mother canning vegetables, ironing the bed sheets and making dinner and desserts from scratch. As I mentioned previously, in our family, being busy was mandatory. Even if your mother worked outside the home, it was likely you witnessed her attempts to continue to provide the same level of care to the family as if it were her only responsibility. Now you may be following that same blueprint. On the other hand, perhaps you felt slighted because your mother did not personally provide certain homemade services and you vowed to make that up to your kids. Either way, many of us hear our mother's voices in our heads and often, the voice is one of disapproval. We have to learn to quiet that voice when it comes to meaningless chores and activities.

I mentioned my mother worked outside the home for a retailer for many years. As a young adult home from college, I vividly remember one year I was talking about the turkey, trimmings and desserts we'd be having over the Thanksgiving holiday. I was shocked when my mother told me she was not making a turkey. Her statement, "Thanksgiving is just another day off to me" blew me away. I failed to understand why my mother would say that about a holiday – especially one that fell on my birthday every few years. Looking back, I realize now that at times, I was a clueless kid!

As I grew older, had a family of my own and took on more responsibility at work, I began to understand her viewpoint. When the burden of preparation falls on a single individual, it is hard to get excited about more work when you know you have to be up at dawn the next day to serve customers on Black Friday. I understand why Mom just wanted to put her feet up and eat pizza in front of the television. I do remember she made a turkey breast that year rather than the whole turkey, and the pies came from the bakery. My family and I enjoyed them enough, and I am glad she forced us to think about what really mattered – family.

As I have mentioned, I love to cook and bake but I do so on my terms and don't let a holiday force me into preparing a meal when I just don't feel like it. Only rarely do I cook a turkey from scratch. Most years, I order take out from the HoneyBaked Ham store or a local restaurant. Either way, everyone enjoys a great meal and their tummies are full.

Has a family member or friend made you feel guilty for not making the kid's lunches or for missing a soccer game? You have to address this issue head on or you will literally stress yourself out and damage your relationships. Seek to understand the cause of your loved one's concern. Maybe this individual is afraid your marriage will suffer if you work outside the home and don't also do all the housework. Maybe she never asked her son to do any housework and her traditional view creates worry in her mind that her son is taking on too much of a burden. Conversely, maybe your father puts pressure on you to attend every one of your child's soccer games because he feels guilty about missing your activities. If a heartfelt discussion does not get you answers to their concerns, then simply and gently set boundaries. Muster up the nerve to tell your father you love your child more than life itself but missing one softball game per season because you travel for work is not going to hurt anyone. It would also be good to mention that it would be great if he would step in for you when you cannot attend.

My sister, Sue, was a stay at home mom and is now a stay at home grandmother. When her children were younger, one of them asked her why she did not work "like Aunt Beth." She very gently reminded her child she could get a job outside the home but if she did, there would be things that she could no longer do for them and then rattled off a list of some of the tasks that would have to fall by the wayside. Her child assimilated the information quickly and never asked the question again.

Kudos to my sister for helping her children understand the tradeoffs between work in and outside the home.

Sometimes perfection really is not the problem. Sometimes we simply refuse to ask for help. Maybe we feel our personal circumstances as a single mother or living in a different city than an immediate family member forces us to go it alone. Perhaps we do not want to be committed to returning the favor when we receive assistance. If total independence is important to you, I ask you to rethink this attitude.

Bees are a part of a colony for a reason. They simply cannot construct a hive, mate, lay eggs and forage for food all on their own. We should not be afraid to seek help either. Asking for help is not a sign of weakness. Conversely, being a martyr doesn't help you or anyone else. We all need help and if you are afraid to rely on the people nearest and dearest to you, ask yourself why. Are they truly not capable of helping you? Do they really extract so much out of you that their assistance does more harm than good? I am not suggesting you leave a child with Uncle Fred the drunk. However, I am suggesting you realistically assess the people that can help you and then establish a support system.

When my son was a baby, I parked in a lot across the river as a means to save money on my commuting costs. A bus would come to the lot and transport us downtown. As you can imagine, I was carrying a kid, a diaper bag and my brief case. In the winter, the extra layering made maneuvering quite difficult. I remember the first time two men on the bus grabbed my son and my bags and helped us onto the bus. I was shocked at the kindness of these men. Their assistance turned into a routine and within a week, my son was on their laps enjoying the short bus ride into town. I learned to tell these men when I would be on vacation so they would not worry that something happened to us. I get tears in my eyes every time I think about how nice those men were to us. They did not have to lift a finger yet they did time and time again, asking nothing in return. If two strangers are willing to help a young mother, do you think your friends and family members would be willing to help you, too?

In Chapter 5, I briefly refer to the idea of swapping services as a means of outsourcing. If your lack of funds or the person helping you is unwilling to accept payment, and this is stopping you from asking for assistance, consider swapping services as a means to pay them back. Agree to take your neighbor's kid to basketball practice if they will agree to watch Leann for an hour each week when you have to stay a little later than usual. If your mother agrees to pick Jerome up from daycare on Wednesdays when you take a class, give her money to order pizza that night so she can focus on your child and not worry about cooking.

Our desire for perfection is in our heads. To get rid of that frame of mind, we have to stop micromanaging, and sweating the small stuff. Instead, be thankful for and take advantage of as much assistance as we can get.

"The bee's life is like a magic well: the more you draw from it the more it fills with water."

Karl Von Frisch

Chapter 11

Pockets of Time

In addition to stopping the less important activities in your life, you should focus on being as efficient as possible with your time. Again, I am not referring to making time to take on more needless tasks, rather how do you use small time slots to knock out important but quick tasks. I refer to these brief respites as "pockets of time." You can accomplish a lot during these tiny windows of time. I once worked with a woman who always carried something to read so when she inevitably had to wait unexpectedly (at the doctor's office, at the airport, etc.) she used this time to catch up on her reading for work and her personal pleasure. Ever since she shared this information with me, I have made it a point to have something to read with me at all times. Kindles, Nooks, tablets and mobile phones make this process even easier today. I drive over three hours each way in a given week commuting to and from my job. I use this time to catch up on work and personal calls and listen to my favorite podcasts or audio books. I really look forward to this time, especially the podcasts and audio books, because I learn something new and it passes the time on an otherwise very long trip.

Pockets of time are opportunities to accomplish much more than just reading. With access to the internet at our fingertips, we can use this time to pay a bill, schedule a hair appointment or call our mother (it is a good idea to be time constrained here). To use these time slots appropriately we have to be prepared, just as my former co-worker did by always having reading material. I keep an ongoing list of tasks I need to complete in a small notebook and I carry it with me all the time. I add tasks as they arise and I cross them off as I complete them. By keeping this notebook handy, I can check my list when I have a free minute or need a break from work and can quickly tackle an item or two. Many organizational phone apps are available and free to use. My husband and I use an app for creating and sharing our grocery list.

Following are examples of some tasks that to complete in small "pockets of time:"

- Schedule your hair or nail appointment (if you have not already scheduled the year in advance).

- Schedule your car or home repair service or window cleaning.

- Schedule your routine doctor and dentist appointments.

- Make a "date night" reservation via Open Table.

- Add something to your grocery list.

- Refill your prescription online or better yet, set it up for auto refill from the onset.

- Do some holiday/birthday/anniversary/ wedding/baby/bridal shower shopping.

- Pay a utility bill, the mortgage, car payment, rent, or put everything you can on automatic debit.

- Check in with a loved one who will be thrilled to hear from you.

- Read.

- Meditate.

- Listen to a podcast while you are exercising, driving, or working around the house.

- Jump online to read the news in between meetings.

- Enjoy your surroundings.

We often think these tasks require large blocks of time, but they really do not need that much time. When you tackle these items a little at a time, they are not quite as daunting as one might think.

For most of us, our tablets and phones will help us knock off the majority of the items on our lists. What if you have things to do that requires more than your phone? Our pets are a good example. If you need to brush the dog, throw the brush into the car and complete this task while your daughter is warming up for a game or waiting for practice to start. Clean your hands with a disinfectant towel and go watch Kayla score a goal! You can run or walk with the dog during intermissions and get in a little exercise.

I am a rabid hockey fan and love my Pittsburgh Penguins. If you have seen the Penguins play on television, you may have seen the "Knitting Lady." She is a Penguins fan who usually gets a seat right behind the coaches and you can see her simultaneously watching the game and knitting. She says it calms her down. This idea of mindless multitasking can help you be more productive.

Here are some other activities you can complete during pockets of time by bringing your tools with you:

- Create a handwritten thank you note or send a birthday card. I always keep a stash on my desks at work and home.

- If you are taking a driving vacation, write out your holiday cards as you are traveling (obviously in the passenger seat). The long road trip allows you the time to write a proper note. Alternatively, start a list of gifts or other tasks that need to complete for the upcoming holiday. Having your spouse or partner engaged gives you the opportunity to talk through and agree upon how you will approach the upcoming event.

- Complete your beauty routine on the run. If you have an early flight, take your flat iron and makeup with you and finish up in the airport restrooms. You get to sleep a little longer and you will look more refreshed when you arrive at your destination.

- Give yourself a facial while you working around the house; just remember not to answer when the doorbell rings!

- Pack your lunch for work while you are making dinner.

- Cut up your veggies for the week while you are watching TV or listening to a podcast.

- Throw in a load of laundry while you are participating in (not leading) a conference call and are working from home.

- Take a walk during a conference call.

- Run outside to get the mail in between meetings when working from home.

- Prepare dinner while participating (again not leading) a conference call. Prep different pieces of the meal throughout the day.

- Do squats or pushups in between meetings or conference calls.

- Take the time to talk with someone face to face or just sit and be in the moment.

Many of us complain we do not have these pockets of time, that we are just so busy we can't manage to squeeze anything else into our hectic schedules. I agree, which is why I suggest you start to squeeze things out. I cannot begin to tell you the countless hours I have spent on Pinterest. The site is addictive! How much time are you spending on Facebook and Twitter? How much time each day do you spend playing online games like Candy Crush or Solitaire? I am not suggesting that you cut these kinds of entertainment out of your lives, but that you set some boundaries allowing yourself a half an hour rather than two hours to play. To prevent time from getting away from you, set your alarm on your phone for 30 minutes and allow yourself that time. When the alarm sounds, shut down the app or the game. I do not allow myself to access this type of entertainment or television until I have completed eighty percent of my "to do" list and I never include these items on my 'to do' list. Your pockets of time are there just waiting for you to discover them.

At work, make meetings twenty-five minutes instead of thirty, forty-five or fifty minutes instead of sixty. Shortening meeting times frees up small pockets of time in which you can fill in with many of the tasks stated herein. When I am making dinner, I put my laptop on the kitchen counter and respond to emails throughout the preparation process. Although it can make for a sticky keyboard at times, I can make progress on reducing the number of emails and feel better about walking away from my computer for the remainder of the evening. Multi-tasking is also a great way to find pockets of time. I usually multi-task when I am chatting with a friend on the phone or via text, but I am also careful to ensure that I am really paying attention to the other person.

"My mind feels like a beehive without the buzz."

Sudheer Reddy

Chapter 12

Investing in You

What are we supposed to do with all this time now that we have organized and prioritized what is important? Let me be clear, de-busying your life will not result in a lot of idle time where you don't know what to do with yourself. Remember, even the Queen Bee does not lounge around doing nothing. She has a job, too! You will always find plenty of activities to fill any void. Stopping the busy-ness will however, help you find time to invest in yourself. It is important to take advantage of down time and insert a litlle "me time." Establishing regular "me time" helps you realize the importance of your own well-being, which further reinforces the need to streamline and stop activities without meaning or value.

"Me time" means you focus on yourself. While that does not always mean you have to be alone, it does require that your well-being is the center of focus. You might want to spend some of your "me time" with a friend, but make sure you are focusing on you and not simply listening to all of her problems. Sometimes I go for a walk and call one of my friends to chat while getting exercise, which results in "me time" and a friendly conversation all in one!

Do not shy away from spending time alone. I find time by myself to be extremely beneficial to decompress. Use this time to clear your head, read a book, listen to music or take a walk. Maybe you choose to sit in a coffee shop and watch strangers come and go. On Sundays I amp up my beauty routine by giving myself a facial and then I sit down and quietly read for a period. Do whatever makes you happy and leaves you feeling de-stressed, highly energized and ready to face the world!

Investing in yourself is important to restoring your well-being. If we are not taking care of ourselves, we cannot take care of anyone or anything else. Think of yourself as an athlete. An athlete spends a great deal of time focused on being her best. She has a routine that pushes her hard, think work and raising a family, but she also realized that to improve she has to step back and give herself a small respite. I encourage you to read the Harvard Business Review article, *The Making of a Corporate Athlete* by Jim Loehr and Tony Schwartz in order to understand how taking care of you is taking care of business.

We need to attend to our own well-being and not just because we will burn ourselves out (which we eventually will), but also because we are not our best selves when we are exhausted. Let's face it; most people who are constantly running on all cylinders and are not getting enough sleep are not fun. They may be short tempered, thoughtless, forgetful or downright mean. Honestly, I used to exhibit many of these traits on a routine basis. I had a list of things that needed to be done (many of them were meaningless) and heaven help anyone or anything that got in the way! I was often sleep deprived and at times, had a surly attitude. I have since learned that lack of sleep is not a badge of honor, rather it is a sign that we are overloaded or not properly prioritizing in our lives.

For years, I was guilty of putting everyone and everything first and this approach negatively affected my health. I did not eat well and the more stressed I was the more bad food I ate. It took me years to realize I would not be of help to anyone if I did not get healthy. Therefore, I finally went back to Weight Watchers and learned new habits. I did this while I was in the middle of caregiving for three older adults along with working full time and traveling. I could have continued to make my busy schedule the reason for not focusing on my health as I did for years, but at some point, the excuses run out.

Invest in your relationships

Second only to investing in yourself is the need to invest in your personal relationships. Without those we love surrounding us, our lives would have little meaning. My husband and I like to take long walks when we are home together. I call this our "debriefing session" because we share all the things that happened over the past week. We talk about what is happening in the news, politics, new ideas, sports, discussing our next vacation and anything else that is on our minds.

I love to listen to my husband share his thoughts and opinions. He is a smart person and simply listening to and learning from him gives me energy.

I find it easier to stay in touch with loved ones by setting a normal routine up for calls. When I am driving home at the end of the week or commuting in at the beginning of the week, I use some of that time to chat with my sister, Sue. This conversation allows me to be current on all family things and it helps deal with some of the boredom of a three-hour drive. My husband and I have a Saturday morning routine with our son where we catch up while he is running errands. We look forward to this call each week and it helps us all stay connected to each other's busy lives. If a loved one is complaining that you are not calling frequently enough, remind them that they can initiate the call as well. Don't forget to give them time slots in which to call. In addition, set a reminder up on your schedule in order to connect more frequently with those that matter the most.

The idea of stopping needless activities is to spend time with those you love. Our kids grow up and move out of the house, our spouses and partners get busy with their own interests. Our parents grow older and we lose them in passing. We must ensure we spend time now with those we love before it is too late.

As adults, we have the need and the right to make decisions about how much we are willing to take on and what we will let go, yet most of us struggle with the latter. Whether it is because we hear our parent's voices in our heads or it is simply easier to take things on ourselves, we simply do too much. We have to slow down and in some cases, stop or we risk being the parent that was not present for the child.

I have worked with Senn Delaney, an organization that consults with corporations on company culture. The people at Senn Delaney have a phrase, "Be here now" that really resonates with me. "Be here now" means you are truly paying attention to what is happening in the moment and you are free from other distractions. It is rare that many of us are present in the moment and our kids and significant others know it. Moreover, we do, too. Both my son and my husband have asked me on more than one occasion, "Are you listening?" Earlier in my career, I had feedback from work colleagues that they thought I was not fully listening to them, but have really tried to change my approach. I am far from perfect but I am present much more than I ever was in the past.

Getting to the point where I could be "in the moment" took a lot of work. If an individual wanted to ask me a quick question while I was on my way to a meeting, I would suggest she walk with me. I thought I was being gracious to squeeze the individual into a packed schedule but it turns out the individual felt rushed and not heard. Now, I stop what I am doing and listen to the question or I ask the individual to contact me at a specific time where I can provide my undivided attention.

At one point in my career, I assumed responsibility for a very large, very public facing program. To say my knowledge of this program was limited was an understatement. For a while, we had 1.5-hour calls every Friday to discuss the program status. I usually work from home on Fridays and when I am not leading a call, I am an avid multi-tasker. However, I knew it was important for me to gain a reasonable understanding of this program so I needed to pay attention. To avoid the temptation of reading and responding to emails during this meeting, I decided to go for a walk each week during this time slot. You might think, "How can she concentrate if she is strolling around the neighborhood?" I found that I could concentrate better if I was walking because I had removed the temptations of multi-tasking. Without a computer in front of me, I was forced to clear my mind and listen to the conversation taking place which in turn helped me not only monitor the progress, but also learn about the program.

Another way I practice being present is to attend the meeting in person. Where I work, we all multi-task, but if someone is standing in front of me presenting then I have a little bit more guilt and I reduce the multi-tasking. I also invite people into my office for meetings. If there are only one or two of us, I sit at the tiny little table, which pulls my attention away from my computer sitting on my desk. After I started this practice, I began to see more and more colleagues showing up in person for these meetings. I am told they showed up because they felt like they were getting much more attention when they were in person rather than when they were on the phone – and they were!

"Doing nothing is better than being busy doing nothing."

Lao Tzu

Chapter 13

Can We Talk?

Throughout this book I have shared many tips to guide you in choices you might consider making as a means to quieting the Busy Bee inside. These tips may seem a bit mundane, but they work. We can only stop unnecessary activity if we tackle the small activities that chip away at our time. I often repeated suggestions intentionally because these areas are some of the biggest time traps. These tips will not be helpful if you don't actually use them. It is the execution I find to be the hardest part. We are encouraged to do more and not less. Based on my own upbringing, the idea that busy is better is in my DNA. Frankly, if I had the choice of growing up with a Busy Bee attitude versus laziness, I would choose Busy Bee every time.

If we want to become a Queen Bee and control our own lives, we have to make choices and trade-offs. We have to outsource required but non-core activities, automate routine tasks and stop doing things that are not essential to living a happy, healthy, fulfilling life.

We must face conflict and have difficult conversations with our friends, co-workers and loved ones so that we can protect our personal hives. We must use tools like preplanning, and be prepared to "just say no" to avoid being coerced into an activity which does not pass the ROM test.

I urge you to step back and take stock of where and who you are. Are you satisfied with your personal and professional life or do you want something more or just different? Do you want to be the Busy Bee or the Queen Bee? While I was a slow learner, I finally caught on. I learned the methods of the Queen Bee and practiced execution in both my personal and professional life and am realizing the fruits of my labor (pass the royal jelly, please)! I am happier and much healthier than I was ten years ago. I have a great career and a family I love and with whom I enjoy spending time. Had I not learned the lessons of the Busy Bee I know I would not be in this positive place. I know it would have been tough to handle both personal and professional challenges. So what is stopping you from taking the steps necessary to free up some time in your personal life and invest in you? Your inner Queen Bee is waiting!

Appendix 1

Activities to outsource or stop

- Cleaning

- Laundry/Dry cleaning

- Lawn maintenance

- Window cleaning

- Flower planting

- Holiday decorating

- Errands

- Tax preparation

- Financial planning, but only if you really need help understanding finances. (Stay very close to it, as you need to know what the other party is doing with your hard-earned money).

- Car washing

- Grocery shopping

- Gift wrapping

- Packing/shipping items

- Pet grooming

- Selling items on eBay

- Walking the dog

- Cooking and/or food prep
- Vacation planning (use a travel agent or a bundled package)
- Baking for bake sales
- Cookie exchanges
- Hosting holiday events
- Shift kid's birthday parties to a restaurant or kid friendly venue
- Cut back on sending holiday cards

Appendix 2

Activities to Automate

- Banking

- Prescription refills

- Bill paying

- Online refills for frequently used goods such as razor blades, paper towel, laundry detergent.

- Enter birthdays, anniversaries and other reoccurring activities on your phone calendar. Preset reminders to schedule certain events like mammograms, eye & dental exams and camp physicals. Make the appointment for the following year if the service provider permits it.

- Order the same gift for multiple people (co-workers, friends, nieces and nephews).

- Schedule nail and hair appointments for the same time each month throughout the year.

- Schedule next year's mammogram at the same time you are receiving your current annual mammogram.

- Road warriors pack a duplicate set of toiletries and keep them with your luggage to save time and ensure you do not accidentally forget something.

Appendix 3

Activities to locate near your home or work or to substitute online ordering:

- Medical and other health professionals, including online doctor visits
- Pharmacies and mail order services for prescriptions and over the counter medication refills
- Grocery stores
- Dry cleaners
- Coffee shops
- Retailers/shopping
- Hair & nail salon
- Books & Movies
- Meal delivery

43256072R00119

Made in the USA
Lexington, KY
26 June 2019